INVENTING BITCOIN

THE TECHNOLOGY BEHIND THE FIRST TRULY SCARCE AND DECENTRALIZED MONEY EXPLAINED

YAN PRITZKER

Get the updated version online at inventingbitcoin.com

Copyright © 2019 by Yan Pritzker.

Cover and illustrations Copyright © 2019 by Nicholas Evans unless otherwise captioned.

All rights reserved.

No part of this book may be reproduced in any form or by any electronic or mechanical means, including information storage and retrieval systems, without written permission from the author, except for the use of brief quotations in a book review.

This book is dedicated to my parents Yury and Lana, who extracted our family from the former USSR, an autocratic socialist regime with tight capital controls.

It's also dedicated to my wife Jessica, who has had to endure my inability to stop talking about Bitcoin, and my staying up late to finish this book.

INTRODUCTION

When many people first hear about Bitcoin, they tend to develop opinions before even attempting to understand it. There is so much noise out there, it's easy to be misled about what Bitcoin is, and how it works. Up until three years ago, I was one of these people.

Why did I decide to write this book? I spent the last twenty years building tech startups. I immerse myself in new technology every day, and I'm pretty good at figuring things out. Even still, it took me five years from first hearing about Bitcoin to actually sitting down to try to understand it. I have a feeling I'm not the only one who could use a little help wrapping their head around this potentially world changing innovation.

I first heard of Bitcoin in 2011 from slashdot.org, a news site for nerds. Back then, the Bitcoin price had gone through the roof to a massive bubble peak of around $30 per coin. All I knew was that some people on the Internet were trying to start some kind of peer to peer payment system. Not knowing the first thing about what it was, how it worked, or anything at all about investing and market cycles, I decided I should buy some just in case it turned out to be important. I had to use a horrible looking site called Mt. Gox to do so. This dollar-to-bitcoin exchange later turned out to be insolvent.

I slowly watched my investment shrink to nearly nothing, as the price crashed from $30 to $2. At some point, I forgot about it completely and went on with my life, working on startups. I don't even know what happened to those coins. I imagine the keys to them are stored on some hard drive from an old laptop, lying in a dump somewhere.

In 2013 I heard about it again. This time, the noise in the media was louder, and now the experience of buying it was a lot slicker. There were apps like Coinbase, which looked downright legitimate. This was a marked improvement from the days of Mt. Gox. It seemed to me that Bitcoin could really be something.

Just in case it was, and again not knowing the first thing about it, I bought at the peak of the bubble (around $1000 per coin) and watched my investment decimated as it fell to about $200 per coin. This time, I figured it wasn't enough money to bother selling, so I left it be, and, proceeded to ignore it as I was knee deep in starting to build my next startup: Reverb.com.

Over the next four years, Reverb grew quickly, becoming the number one destination for musicians. I was making a difference in the world and bringing music to people. I was the CTO of an exciting, fast growing tech company, doing something I was passionate about, and I had no time for silly Internet money.

I'm embarrassed to say that it wasn't until the summer of 2016 that I finally watched my first video by Andreas Antonopoulos, which finally forced me to sit up and pay attention. I started asking questions. Where does Bitcoin come from? Who controls it? How does it work? What is mining? What impact will it have on the world? I started reading everything I could get my hands on, listening to hours of podcasts and videos every day for a year and a half straight.

Finally, in early 2018, just after Bitcoin hit another all time high at around $20,000 per coin, I decided to leave Reverb in pursuit of helping bring Bitcoin to the world in whatever way I could. Why did I leave my very successful startup to work on Bitcoin? I believe that the invention of Bitcoin is the kind of thing that comes around once in a lifetime; perhaps once in many lifetimes.

If Bitcoin succeeds, it may prove to be as important as the printing press (decentralized production of information), the Internet (decentralized content and communication), and three-branch democracy (decentralized government). I hope that by understanding how Bitcoin works, you'll understand how it can turn out to be a force for good in the world. Bitcoin will decentralize the production and consumption of money, which is the key to unlocking new ways for humanity to collaborate on a scale that was previously unimaginable.

The price of Bitcoin is mostly what you hear about in the media. One day it's going to a million dollars, and the next it's in a death spiral going to zero. It's either that or Bitcoin will use all the world's energy and destroy the planet within ten years. Of course this is false, and hopefully you'll understand why once you learn about how it works. You'll also understand why price bubbles are one of the least interesting things about Bitcoin.

My goal with this book isn't to analyze the economics of Bitcoin and sound money, though we'll touch on these concepts briefly. I'm not going to look at Bitcoin from the standpoint of investing, or try to convince you that everyone should own a little. I would highly recommend *The Bitcoin Standard* by Saifedean Ammous as an immediate follow-up to this book if you haven't read it already.

We're also not going to dig into any computer code, and no computer science background is required to understand this book. If you want to look at Bitcoin through that lens, I recommend the seminal *Mastering Bitcoin* by Andreas Antonopoulos, and the newly released *Programming Bitcoin* by Jimmy Song.

For me, understanding all the things that come together to make Bitcoin work was a profound moment. In this book, I hope to share that knowledge with you in a short, simple format. My goal today is to tickle your brain, and to give you a taste of the computer science, economics, and game theory that make Bitcoin one of the most interesting and profound inventions of our time. By understanding the workings of Bitcoin, I hope you will find, like I did, that Bitcoin is much deeper than it appears to be at first, and may have an incredible impact on the world for generations to come.

The way we'll do it is one step at a time. With nothing but a high school level math background, we will walk through *inventing bitcoin*, step by step. I hope that this book will give you just enough of an introduction to send you down the Bitcoin rabbit hole. Let's get started!

1
WHAT IS BITCOIN?

Bitcoin is a *peer to peer electronic cash*, a new form of digital money that can be transferred between people or computers without any trusted middleman (such as a bank), and whose issuance is not under the control of any single party.

Think of a paper dollar or physical metal coin. When you give that money to another person, they don't need to know who you are. They just need to trust that the cash they get from you is not a forgery. Typically people do this with physical money using just their eyes and fingers, or using special testing equipment for larger amounts.

As we've shifted to a digital society, the majority of our payments are now made over the Internet by means of a middleman service: a credit card company like Visa, a digital payment provider such as PayPal or Apple Pay, or an online platform like WeChat in China.

The movement toward digital payments brings with it the reliance on a central actor that has to approve and verify every payment. This is because the nature of money has changed from a physical thing you can carry, transfer, and verify yourself, to digital bits that have to be stored and verified by a third party that controls their transfer.

As we give up our cash for convenient digital payments, we also create a system where we give extraordinary powers to those who would seek to oppress us. Digital payment platforms have become the basis of dystopian authoritarian systems of control such as those used by the Chinese government in order to monitor dissidents and prevent citizens whose behavior they don't like from purchasing goods and services.

Bitcoin offers an alternative to centrally controlled digital money with a system that gives us back the person to person nature of cash, but in a digital form:

1. A digital asset (typically *bitcoin* with a lowercase *b*) whose supply is limited, known in advance, and unchangeable. This stands in stark contrast to the paper notes and digital versions thereof issued by governments and central banks, whose supply expands at an unpredictable rate.
2. A bunch of interconnected computers (the *Bitcoin network*), which anyone can join by running a piece of software. This network serves to issue bitcoins, track their ownership, and transfer them between participants without relying on any middlemen such as banks, payment companies, and government entities.
3. The Bitcoin client software, a piece of code that anyone can run on their computer to become a participant in the network. This software is open source, which means that anyone can see how it works, as well as contribute new features and bug fixes to it.

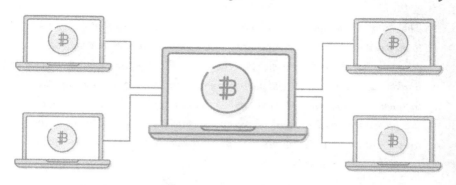

Bitcoin is a network of computers running the Bitcoin client software.

We'll get into the motivations behind Bitcoin in the next section.

Where Did It Come From?

Bitcoin was invented by a person or group known by the pseudonym of Satoshi Nakamoto around 2008. No one knows the identity of this person or group, and as far as we know, they've disappeared and haven't been heard from for years.

On Feb 11, 2009, Satoshi wrote about an early version of Bitcoin on an online forum for *cypherpunks*, people who work on cryptography technology and are concerned with individual privacy and freedom. Though this isn't the first official release announcement of Bitcoin, it does contain a good summary of Satoshi's motivations, so we'll use it to lay the ground work for our discussion.

The relevant bits are extracted below. In the next section, we'll walk through some of these statements and try to understand what problems of the current financial system Satoshi was solving:

> I've developed a new open source P2P e-cash system called Bitcoin. It's completely decentralized, with no central server or trusted parties, because everything is based on crypto proof instead of trust. [...]

The root problem with conventional currency is all the trust that's required to make it work. The central bank must be trusted not to debase the currency, but the history of fiat currencies is full of breaches of that trust. Banks must be trusted to hold our money and transfer it electronically, but they lend it out in waves of credit bubbles with barely a fraction in reserve. We have to trust them with our privacy, trust them not to let identity thieves drain our accounts. Their massive overhead costs make micropayments impossible.

A generation ago, multi-user time-sharing computer systems had a similar problem. Before strong encryption, users had to rely on password protection to secure their files [...]

Then strong encryption became available to the masses, and trust was no longer required. Data could be secured in a way that was physically impossible for others to access, no matter for what reason, no matter how good the excuse, no matter what.

It's time we had the same thing for money. With e-currency based on cryptographic proof, without the need to trust a third party middleman, money can be secure and transactions effortless. [...]

Bitcoin's solution is to use a peer-to-peer network to check for double-spending. In a nutshell, the network works like a distributed timestamp server, stamping the first transaction to spend a coin. It takes advantage of the nature of information being easy to spread but hard to stifle. For details on how it works, see the design paper at http://www.bitcoin.org/bitcoin.pdf

— SATOSHI NAKAMOTO

What Problems Does it Solve?

Let's break down some of Satoshi's post. Throughout the book, we will cover how these concepts are actually implemented. Don't worry if something feels unfamiliar in this section, as we'll cover it in depth later. The idea here is to see Satoshi's goals so that we can aim to achieve them as we go through the exercise of *Inventing Bitcoin*.

> *I've developed a new open source P2P e-cash system*

P2P stands for *peer to peer* and indicates a system where one person can interact with another without anyone in the middle, as equal peers. You may recall P2P file sharing technologies like Napster, Kazaa, and BitTorrent, which first enabled people to share music and movies with each other without a middleman. Satoshi designed Bitcoin to allow people to exchange *e-cash*, electronic cash, without going through a middleman in much the same way.

The software is *open source*, which means that anyone can see how it works and contribute to it. This is important as it removes the requirement to trust Satoshi. We don't need to believe anything Satoshi wrote in his post about how the software works. We can look at the code and verify how it works for ourselves. Furthermore, we can evolve the functionality of the system by changing the code.

> *It's completely decentralized, with no central server or trusted parties...*

Satoshi mentions that the system is *decentralized* to distinguish it from systems that do have central control. Prior attempts to create digital cash such as DigiCash by David Chaum were backed by a *central server*, a computer or set of computers that was responsible for issuance and payment verification, under the control of one corporation.

Such centrally controlled private money schemes were doomed to failure; people can't rely on a money that can disappear when the company goes out of business, gets hacked, suffers a server crash, or is shut down by the government.

Bitcoin, on the other hand, is not run and controlled by a single company, but rather by a network of individuals and companies all over the world. To shut down Bitcoin would require shutting down tens to hundreds of thousands of computers around the world, many in undisclosed locations. It would be a hopeless game of wack-a-mole as any attack of this nature would simply encourage the creation of new Bitcoin *nodes,* or computers on the network.

> *...everything is based on crypto proof instead of trust*

The Internet, and indeed most modern computer systems, are built on cryptography, a method of obscuring information so that only the recipient of the information can decode it. How does Bitcoin get rid of the requirement of *trust?* We'll dive into this later in the book, but the basic idea is that instead of trusting someone that says "I am Alice" or "I have $10 in my account," we can use cryptographic math to state the same facts in a way that is very easy to verify by the recipient of the proof but impossible to forge. Bitcoin uses cryptographic math throughout its design to allow participants to check the behavior of everyone else without trusting any central party.

> *We have to trust [the banks] with our privacy, trust them not to let identity thieves drain our accounts*

Unlike using your bank account, digital payment system, or credit card, Bitcoin allows two parties to transact without giving up any personally identifying information. Centralized repositories of consumer data stored at banks, credit card companies, payment processors, and governments are giant honeypots for hackers. As if to prove Satoshi's point, Equifax was massively compromised in 2017, leaking the identities and financial data of more than 140 million people to hackers.

Bitcoin decouples financial transactions from real world identities. After all, when we give physical cash to someone, they don't need to know who we are, nor do we need to worry that after our exchange they can use some information we gave them to steal more of our money. Why shouldn't we expect the same, or better, from digital money?

> *The central bank must be trusted not to debase the currency, but the history of fiat currencies is full of breaches of that trust*

Fiat, which is Latin for "let it be done," refers to government and central-bank issued currency which is decreed as legal tender by the government. Historically, money was created from things that were hard to produce, easy to verify, and easy to transport, such as seashells, glass beads, silver, and gold. Any time something was used as money, there was a temptation to create more of it. If someone came along with superior technology for quickly creating lots of something, that thing lost value. This is how European settlers were able to strip the African continent of its wealth, by trading easy for them to produce glass beads for hard to produce human slaves. This is why gold was considered such a good money for so long—it was hard to produce more of it quickly. [1]

We slowly shifted from a world economy that used gold as money to one where paper certificates were issued as a claim on that gold. Eventually, the paper was entirely separated from any physical backing by Nixon, who ended the international convertibility of the US dollar to gold in 1971.

The end of the gold standard allowed governments and central banks full permission to increase the money supply at will, diluting the value of each note in circulation, known as *debasement*. Although government-issued, redeemable for nothing, pure fiat currency is the money we all know and use day to day, it is actually a relatively new experiment in the scope of world history.

We must trust our governments not to abuse their printing press, but we don't need to look far for examples of *breaches of that trust*. In autocratic and centrally planned regimes where the government has their finger directly on the money machine, such as Venezuela, the currency has become nearly worthless. The Venezuelan Bolivar went from 2 Bolivar to the U.S. dollar in 2009 to 250,000 Bolivar to the U.S. dollar in 2019. As I write this book, Venezuela is in the process of collapse due to the terrible mismanagement of its economy by its government.

Satoshi wanted to offer an alternative to *fiat* currency whose supply is always expanding unpredictably. In order to prevent *debasement*, Satoshi designed a system of money where the supply was fixed and issued at a predictable and unchangeable rate. There will only ever be 21 million bitcoins, though each bitcoin can be divided into 100 million units now called satoshis, producing a final total of 2.1 quadrillion satoshis in circulation around the year 2140.

Prior to Bitcoin, it was not possible to prevent a digital asset from being infinitely reproduced. It is cheap and easy to copy a digital book, audio file, or video and send it to your friend. The only exceptions to this are digital assets controlled by middlemen. For example, when you rent a movie from iTunes, you can watch it on your device only because iTunes controls the delivery of the movie and can stop it after your rental period. Similarly, your digital money is controlled by your bank. It is the bank's job to keep a record of how much money you have, and if you transfer it to someone else, they can authorize or deny such a transfer.

Bitcoin is the first digital system which enforces scarcity without any middlemen and is the first asset known to humanity whose unchangeable supply and schedule of issuance is known completely in advance. Not even precious metals like gold have this property, since we can always mine more and more gold if it is profitable to do so. Imagine discovering an asteroid containing ten times as much gold as we have on earth. What would happen to the price of gold given such abundant supply? Bitcoin is immune to such discoveries and supply manipulations. It is simply impossible to produce more of it, and we'll explain why in later chapters.

The nature of money and the workings of the existing monetary system are intricate, and this book will not cover them in depth. If you would like to know more about the fundamentals of money as they apply to Bitcoin, I would recommend *The Bitcoin Standard* by Saifedean Ammous as a starting point.

> *Data could be secured in a way that was physically impossible for others to access, no matter for what reason, no matter how good the excuse, no matter what. [...] It's time we had the same thing for money*

Our current systems of securing money, such as putting it in a bank, rely on trusting someone else to do the job. Trusting such a middleman not only requires confidence that they won't do something malicious or foolish, but also that the government won't seize or freeze your funds by exerting pressure on this middleman. However, it has been demonstrated time and time again, that governments can and do shut down access to money when they feel threatened.

It might sound silly to someone living in the United States, or another highly regulated economy, to contemplate waking up with your money gone, but it happens all the time. I've had my funds frozen by PayPal simply because I hadn't used my account in months. It took me over a week to get restored access to "my" money. I'm lucky to live in the United States, where at least I could hope to seek some legal relief if PayPal froze my funds, and where I have basic trust that my government and bank won't steal my money.

Much worse things have happened, and are currently happening, in countries with less freedom, such as banks shutting down during currency collapses in Greece, banks in Cyprus proposing bail-ins to confiscate funds from their customers, or the government declaring certain bank notes worthless in India.

The former USSR, where I grew up, had a government controlled economy leading to massive shortages of goods. It was illegal to own foreign currencies such as the US dollar. When we wanted to leave, we could only exchange a limited amount of money per person to US dollars under an official government mandated exchange rate that was vastly divorced from the true free market rate. Effectively, the government stripped us of what little wealth we had by keeping an iron grip on the economy and the movement of capital.

Autocratic countries tend to implement strict economic controls, preventing people from withdrawing their money from banks, carrying it out of the country, or exchanging it for not-yet-worthless currencies like the US dollar on the free market. This allows the government free reign to implement insane economic experiments such as the socialist system of the USSR.

Bitcoin does not rely on trust in a third party to secure your money. Instead Bitcoin makes your coins *impossible for others to access* without a special key that only you hold, *no matter for what reason, no matter how good the excuse, no matter what*. By holding Bitcoin, you hold the keys to your own financial freedom. Bitcoin separates money and state

> Bitcoin's solution is to use a peer-to-peer network to check for double-spending [...] like a distributed timestamp server, stamping the first transaction to spend a coin

A *network* refers to the idea that a bunch of computers are connected and can send messages to each other. The word *distributed* means that there is not a central party in control, but rather that all the participants coordinate to make the network successful.

In a system without central control, it's important to know that nobody is cheating. The idea of *double-spending* refers to the ability to spend the same money twice. This is not a problem with physical money as it leaves your hand when you spend it. Digital transactions, however, can be copied just like music or movies. When you send money through a bank, they make sure that you can't move the same money twice. In a system without central control, we need a way to prevent this kind *double-spending*, which is effectively the same as forging money.

Satoshi is describing that the participants of the Bitcoin network work together to *timestamp* (put in order) transactions so that we know what came first, and therefore we can reject any future attempts to spend the same money. In the next few chapters, we will build this system from the ground up. It will enable us to detect forgery without relying on any central issuer or transaction validator.

Bitcoin was not an invention made in a vacuum. In his paper, Satoshi cited several important attempts at implementing similar systems including Wei Dai's b-money, and Adam Back's Hashcash. The invention of Bitcoin stood on the shoulders of giants, but no one prior had put all the right pieces together, creating the first system for issuing and transferring a truly scarce digital money without central control.

Satoshi tackled a number of interesting technical problems in order to address the issues of privacy, debasement, and central control in current monetary systems:

1. How to create a peer to peer network that allows anyone to voluntarily join and participate.
2. How a group of people that don't have to reveal their identities or trust each other can maintain a shared ledger of value, even if some of them are dishonest.
3. How to allow people to issue their own unforgeable currency without relying on a central issuer while maintaining the

scarcity of that currency so that production of new units isn't a free-for-all.

When Bitcoin was launched, only a handful of people used it and ran the Bitcoin software on their computer *nodes* to power the Bitcoin network. Most people at the time thought it was a joke, or that the system would reveal serious design flaws that would make it unworkable.

Over time, more people joined the network, using their computers to add security to the network and reinforcing that it had value by exchanging other currencies for it, or accepting it for goods and services. Today, ten years later, it is used by millions of people with tens to hundreds of thousands of nodes running the free Bitcoin software, which is developed by hundreds of volunteers and companies worldwide.

Let's figure out how we can build this system!

---

1. For a great overview of monetary history, I recommend the essay *Shelling Out* by Nick Szabo: https://nakamotoinstitute.org/shelling-out/

2
REMOVING THE MIDDLEMAN

In the prior chapter, we discussed that Bitcoin provides a peer to peer system for the transfer of value. Before we can dive into how that works, let's first understand how a traditional bank or payment company deals with tracking asset ownership and transfers.

Banks are Just Ledgers

How does a digital payment made by your bank, PayPal, or ApplePay work? Very simply, these middlemen act as glorified ledgers of accounts and transfers.

The purpose of a bank is to store your deposits and to guard them. But deposits these days are primarily electronic, rather than coins or paper. As such, the job of a bank is now to maintain and guard a database of accounts. Since the data is electronic, the security guards are also mostly electronic. Banks use software intrusion detection systems, backups to guard against data loss, third party audits to make sure their internal processes aren't compromised, and insurance to bail them out in case something goes wrong.

Here is how they work. In this example, we will say *bank* but we really mean any other party that processes payments. We start with a ledger of accounts that shows that Alice and Bob deposited money with the bank.

Bank's Ledger

1. Alice: Credit for Cash Deposit +$2
2. Bob: Credit for Cash Deposit +$10

When Alice wants to send $2 to Bob, she calls her bank or uses a web or mobile wallet produced by her bank, authenticates herself to the bank using a username and password or pin code, and then puts in the request to transfer. The bank records it in their ledger.

Bank's Ledger

1. Alice: Credit for Cash Deposit +$2
2. Bob: Credit for Cash Deposit +$10
3. Alice: Debit -$2
4. Bob: Credit +$2

So the bank has recorded the new debits and credits, and now the money has moved.

The Double-Spending Problem

What happens if Alice now tries to spend those two dollars again? This is called the Double-Spending Problem. She files the request to the bank, but the bank says "Sorry, we see you've already spent $2 to pay Bob. You have no more money to send."

When you have a central authority like a bank, it is very easy for the bank to tell that you're trying to spend the cash you've already spent. That's because they're the only ones that get to modify the ledger, and they have internal processes including backup systems and audits by computers and humans to make sure it's correct and hasn't been tampered with.

We call this a *centralized* system because it has a single point of control.

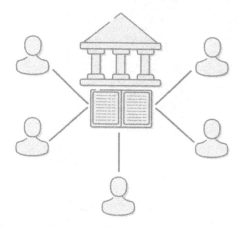

The bank stores a ledger that everyone can access, but only by going through the bank.

Distributing the Ledger

The first problem Bitcoin aims to solve is the removal of a trusted middleman by creating a *peer to peer* system. Let's imagine that banks have gone away and we need to recreate our financial system. How can we maintain a ledger without any central party?

If we don't have one central ledger, it must be the case that the ledger now belongs to the people. Vive la révolution. Here's how we do it.

First, a bunch of us get together and create a *network*. This just means we have some way to talk to each other. Let's say we exchange phone numbers or Snapchat accounts. When Alice wants to send money to Bob, instead of calling the bank, she tells all her friends: "I'm sending $2 to Bob." Everyone acknowledges, replying "cool, we got it," and writes it into their own copy of the ledger. The picture now looks like this:

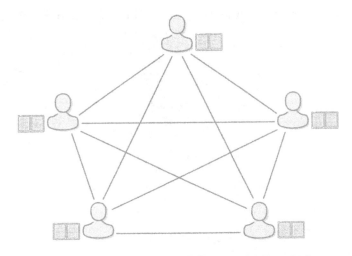

Everyone has a copy of the ledger they can access independently.

So now, instead of a single bank, we have a copy of the ledger in everyone's hands. Every time someone wants to spend money, they simply have to tell all their friends. Everyone records the transactions. Since the ledger is no longer in one place, we call it *distributed,* and because no central party is in charge, we call it *decentralized*. This solves the problem of removing the middleman.

Now that we have no middleman, how will we deal with double-spends? Who will we consult instead of the bank to verify whether the money being spent hasn't already been spent? Since everyone has a copy of the ledger, it must be the case that we have to consult everyone. This system is called *consensus*-based because it relies on everyone agreeing on a particular version of the truth.

If Alice tries to re-spend the $2 she already sent to Bob, her transaction would be rejected by everyone on the network, since they would consult their ledgers and tell her that according to their records, she already spent the money. Therefore, they would not record her second attempt to spend money she already spent. We now have a peer to peer consensus network for recording ownership and transfers of funds.

As long as our distributed ledger requires *permission* to join, and we can *trust* every party to be honest, the system works. But this kind of design can't scale to be used by millions of people worldwide. Distributed systems made of arbitrary participants are inherently unreliable. Some people might occasionally go offline. That means they may not hear about our transactions when we broadcast them. Others may be actively trying to defraud us by saying that certain transactions happened or didn't happen. New people may join the network and get conflicting copies of the ledger.

Let's take a look at how someone might try to cheat.

The Double-Spend Attack

If I'm Alice, I can *collude* with some of the other folks and tell them: "when I spend money, don't write it into your ledgers. Pretend like it never happened." Here's how Alice can perform a Double Spend Attack.

Starting with a balance of $2, Alice does the following:

1. She sends her $2 to Bob, to buy a candy bar. Now she should have $0 left.
2. David, Eve, and Farrah are colluding with Alice and do not write the transaction from Alice to Bob into their ledgers. In their copy, Alice never spent her money and still has a balance of $2.
3. Charlotte is an honest ledger keeper. She notes the transaction from Alice to Bob. In her ledger, Alice has $0.
4. Henry was on vacation for a week and hasn't heard about any of these transactions. He joins the network and asks for a copy of the ledger.

5. Henry gets 4 false copies (David, Eve, Farrah, Alice) and one honest copy (Charlotte). How does he determine which one is real? With no better system, he trusts the majority of participants and is duped into accepting the fake ledger as the correct one.
6. Alice buys a candy bar from Henry using the $2 she doesn't actually have. Henry accepts it because for all he knows, Alice still has $2 in her account according to the ledger he got from everyone else.
7. Alice now has 2 candy bars, and $4 of fake money has been created in the system. She pays off her friends in candy bars, and they repeat the attack 100 times on every new person who joins the network.
8. Alice is now holding all the candy bars and everyone else is holding large bags of fake money.
9. When they try to spend the money Alice supposedly sent them, David, Eve, and Farrah who control the majority of the network, reject these spends because they know the money is fake to begin with.

This is called a *consensus failure*. The people in the network did not come to consensus on what the state of reality is. Having no better system, they went with majority rule, which led to dishonest people controlling the network and spending money they didn't have.

If we want to make a *permissionless* system where anyone can participate without asking, then it must also be resilient to dishonest actors.

Solving the Distributed Consensus Problem

Now we get to solve one of the hardest problems in computer science: distributed consensus between parties where some are dishonest or unreliable. This problem is known as the Byzantine Generals Problem and is the key that Satoshi Nakamoto used to unlock the invention of Bitcoin. We need to get a bunch of people to agree on the entries in the ledger without knowing which ledger keepers have been writing down all the transactions correctly and honestly.

One naive solution is simply to appoint honest ledger keepers. Instead of everyone getting to write to the ledger, we pick a handful of friends like Charlotte, Gary, Frank, and Zoe to do it, because they don't tell lies and everyone knows they never party on the weekends.

So every time we have to process a transaction, instead of telling all our friends, we just call up Charlotte and the gang. They're happy to maintain the ledger for us for a small fee. After they write to the ledger, they call everyone else and tell them about the new ledger entries, which everyone still keeps as backup.

This system works really well, except one day, government agents show up and they want to know who's been running this shadow financial system. They arrest Charlotte and friends and take them away, putting an end to our distributed ledger. We all have unreliable backups, can't trust each other, and can't figure out whose backup should be used to start a new system.

Instead of a full shutdown, the government can also threaten our ledger keepers quietly with jail time if they accept transactions to Alice (who is suspected of selling drugs). The system is now effectively under central control and we can't call it permissionless anymore.

What if we try democracy? Let's find a pool of 50 honest people and we'll run elections every day to keep rotating who gets to write to the ledger. Everyone in the network gets a vote.

This system works great until people show up and use violence or financial coercion to achieve the same ends as before:

1. Coerce the electorate to vote for the ledger keepers of their choosing.

2. Coerce the elected ledger keepers to write fake entries into the ledger or prevent certain transactions from processing.

We have a problem. Any time we appoint specific people to maintain the ledger, they must be trusted to be honest, and we have no way of defending them from being coerced by someone to do dishonest deeds and corrupting our ledger.

Mistaken Identity and Sybil Attacks

So far we looked at two failed methods of ensuring honesty: one used specific known ledger keepers, and the other used elected and rotating ledger keepers. The failure of both systems was that the basis of our trust was tied to real-world identity: we still had to specifically identify the individuals that would be responsible for our ledger. Whenever we assume trust based on identity, we open ourselves up to something called a Sybil Attack. This is basically a fancy name for impersonation; it's named after a woman with multiple personality disorder.

Have you ever received a weird text from one of your friends only to find out her phone had been hijacked? When it comes to billions or even trillions of dollars at stake, people will justify all kinds of violence in order to steal that phone and send that text. It is imperative that we prevent the people who get to keep our ledger for us from being coerced in any way. How do we do this?

Let's Build a Lottery

If we don't want the possibility of people being compromised by threats of violence or bribery, we need a system with so many participants that it would be impractical for anyone to coerce them. Even better, we don't want to know their identities at all. It must be the case that anyone at all can participate in our system, and that we don't have to introduce any kind of voting, which is subject to coercion by violence and vote buying.

What if we ran a lottery where we picked someone at random every time we wanted to write to the ledger? Here's our first design draft:

1. Anyone at all in the world can participate. Tens of thousands of people can join our ledger keeper lottery network.
2. When we want to send money, we announce to the entire network the transactions we want to perform, just like we did before.
3. Instead of having everyone write down the transactions, we hold a lottery to see who will win the right to enter these transactions into the ledger.
4. When we select a winner, that person gets to write all the transactions that they just heard about into the ledger.
5. If the person writes *valid* transactions into the ledger that play by the rules enforced by all other participants, they are paid a fee.
6. Everyone maintains a copy of the ledger, adding the information that the latest lottery winner produced.
7. We wait for a while so that most people have time to update their ledger to the latest entry, and then run the lottery again.

This system is an improvement. It's impractical to compromise the participants of this system because it's impossible to know who the participants are, and who the next winner will be.

However, we have no clear answer for how to run this lottery without someone in charge, or why we should trust that the winner would act honestly when writing to the ledger. We'll figure out how to solve that next.

3
PROOF OF WORK

The lottery system as designed so far has two major problems:

1. Who will sell the tickets to the lottery and pick the winning numbers, if we have already determined that we can't have any kind of central trusted party?
2. How do we ensure that the winner of the lottery actually writes good transactions into the ledger rather than trying to cheat the rest of us?

If we want a *permissionless* system that anyone can join, then we have to remove the requirement of trust from the system and make our system *trustless*. We have to come up with a system that has the following properties:

1. It must be possible for everyone to generate their own lottery ticket, since we can't trust a central authority. Standard centralized lottery systems like Powerball are run by someone generating a bunch of tickets with random numbers on them. Since we can't rely on central authority, we must allow anyone to generate their own ticket numbers.

2. We must have some way to make playing the lottery cost something so that we can prevent someone from monopolizing the lottery by generating a huge number of tickets for free. How do we make it so that you actually have to spend money to buy tickets when there is no one you can buy them from? We'll make you buy them from the universe by burning electricity, a costly resource.
3. It must be easy for all other participants to verify that you've won the lottery solely by examining your ticket. In Powerball, the lottery operators generate the winning combo. Since we can't have that in a decentralized system, we can instead have everyone agree on a number range ahead of time, and if your lottery number falls within the range, you win the lottery. We'll use a cryptographic trick called a hash function to do this.

Proof of Work: an Energy Intensive Asymmetric Puzzle

The elegant solution to all three of these problems is called Proof of Work. It was actually invented way before Bitcoin, in 1993. The full explanation of how this lottery works is probably the hardest thing to understand about Bitcoin, so we'll devote the next few chapters to covering the solution in depth.

We need to make it expensive to "buy tickets" to the lottery, otherwise people could generate an unlimited number of tickets. What's something that is guaranteed to be expensive, but doesn't have to come from any central authority?

This is where physics plays into Bitcoin: the first law of thermodynamics says that energy can neither be created nor destroyed. In other words, there's no such thing as a free lunch when it comes to energy. Electricity is always expensive because you have to purchase it from the power producers, or run your own power plant. In either case, obtaining electricity is costly.

The concept behind Proof of Work is that you participate in a random process, similar to rolling a die. But instead of a six sided die, this one has about as many sides as there are atoms in the universe. In order to roll the die and generate lottery numbers, your computer must perform operations that cost you in terms of electricity.

To win the lottery, you must produce a number which is mathematically derived from the transactions you want to write to the ledger plus the value of the die you rolled. In order to find this winning number, you may have to roll this die billions, trillions, or quadrillions of times, burning thousands of dollars worth of energy. Since the process is based on randomness, it is possible for everyone to generate their own lottery tickets without a central authority using just a random number generating computer and a list of transactions they want to write to the ledger.

Even though it may have taken you thousands of dollars to burn enough energy to find a winning random number, in order for everyone else on the network to validate that you're a winner, they need to perform only a few basic checks:

1. Is the number you provided less than a Target Number range everyone agreed upon ahead of time?
2. Is the number indeed mathematically derived from a valid set of transactions that you want to write to the ledger?
3. Are the transactions you are presenting valid by the rules of Bitcoin: not double spending, not generating new Bitcoin outside an allowed schedule, etc.

Proof of Work is a random chance process that requires many computations to find a winning number. However, it only takes a single operation to verify the solution. Think of it like a crossword puzzle or a sudoku. It might take a long time to solve, but anyone given the answers and the clues can validate it quickly. This makes the Proof of

Work system *asymmetric:* it's hard for the players but easy for the validators.

Because you've burned a considerable amount of energy and therefore money playing this lottery, you want everyone to accept your winning lottery ticket. Thus, you are incentivized to behave well by writing only valid transactions into the ledger.

If you, for example, try to spend money that's already been spent, then your "winning" lottery ticket will be rejected by everyone else, and you'll lose all the money you spent buying the energy to burn for the ticket. On the other hand, if you write valid transactions into the ledger, we'll reward you in bitcoin so you can pay your energy bills and keep some profit.

The Proof of Work system has an important property of being *real world costly*. Thus, if you wanted to attack the network by coercing some of its participants, you'd have to not only come to their house and take over their computer, but you'd also have to pay their electrical bills.

How do participants prove they've burned this energy? We'll need a quick Computer Science primer on two concepts: hashing and bits.

Hashing

Bitcoin's asymmetric Proof of Work puzzle involves using a *hash function*. From basic algebra, we know that a function is a box where you put in an *input* value x and you get an *output* value $f(x)$. For example, the function $f(x)=2x$ takes a value and multiplies it by two. So the input $x=2$ gives us the output $f(x)=4$.

A hash function is a special function, where you put in any string of letters, numbers, or other data, like "Hello world", and you get out a giant random looking number:

111181171325821924266132935775749045845548904466436160011265843466335415020 95

The particular hash function I used to hash "Hello world" is called sha256 and happens to be the one Bitcoin uses.

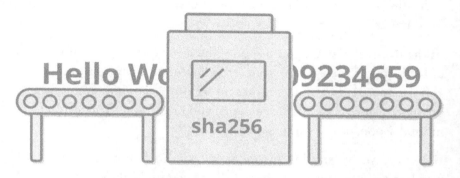

Data goes in one side, giant unpredictable numbers come out the other.

The sha256 hash function has the following properties that are useful to us:

1. The output is deterministic: you always get the same output for the same input.
2. The output is unpredictable: changing just one letter or adding a space to the input string will drastically change the output, so much so that you cannot find any correlation to the original input.
3. It is quick to compute the hash for any size of input data.
4. It is infeasible to find two strings that hash to the same output.
5. Given the output hash of sha256, it is impossible to arrive back at the input string. We call this a one-way function.
6. The output is always a specific size (256 *bits* for sha256).

A Quick Primer on Bits

The number system you know and love, comprised of the numbers 0 through 9 is called *decimal* because it has ten digits. Computers, on the other hand, prefer a different number system made of ones and zeros, indicating the presence or absence of an electrical signal. This number system is called *binary*.

In the decimal system, you use only the *digits* 0 through 9. If you use only one digit you can represent ten different numbers, 0 through 9. If you use two digits, you can represent 10 x 10 = 100 different numbers: 00, 01, ... through 99. For three digits, you can have 10 x 10 x 10 = 1000 numbers: 000, 001, ... through 999.

Hopefully you're starting to see a pattern. To figure out how big a number we can represent with N digits, we multiply ten by itself N times, in other words 10^N, or 10 to the power of N.

Binary works the same way. The only thing that changes is the number of digits that are available to us. While we're used to decimal with ten digits, a *binary digit* or *bit* can only have two values: zero and one.

If 1 bit can represent two values, then two bits can represent 4 values: 00, 01, 10, 11. You can calculate this by multiplying 2 x 2 since each digit can have two values.

Three bits can represent 2 x 2 x 2 = 2^3 = 8 values, which are 000, 001, 010, 011, 100, 101, 110, 111.

A *binary* number that is N *bits* long can represent 2^N different values.

Therefore, the number of unique values you can represent with 256 bits, the size of the sha256 hashing function, is 2^{256}. That's a giant, almost inconceivable number. Represented in decimal, this number is 78 digits long. To put this in perspective, it's in the same ballpark as the estimated number of atoms in the known universe.

2^{256} = 115,792,089,237,316,195,423,570,985,008,687,907,
853,269,984,665,640,564,039,457,584,007,913,129,639,936

This is the number of possible outputs when you hash any string with sha256 hash function. Thus, it is effectively impossible to predict what the number produced by this function will look like. It would be like predicting 256 coin tosses in a row, or guessing the location of a specific atom that I've picked somewhere in the universe.

This number is too long to keep writing out, so we'll just say 2^{256} from now on, but I hope that this triggers a mental image of a universe of possibilities for you.

Let's Hash Some Strings

Here are some example strings and their sha256 hashes. I've shown their output as decimal numbers, though inside a computer these would appear as a binary string of ones and zeros.

The point here is to demonstrate how drastically the number changes based on a small change to the input string. You can't predict the output produced by the hash function based on what you put into it:

"Hello world!"
52740724284578854442640185928423074974
81806529570658746454048816174655413720

"Hello world!!"
95863319874939535731602344194643497258374513872780665335270495834770720452323

There's no way for anyone, not even a computer, to look at the resulting random looking number and figure out the string that created it. If you want to play with sha256, you can try it out at https://passwordsgenerator.net/sha256-hash-generator.

Hashing to Win the Proof of Work Lottery

Now we're ready to talk about the key bit of magic. We said there are 2^{256} total possible sha256 output values. To make it easier to understand, let's pretend that there are only a total of 1000 possible hash outputs.

The lottery system works like this:

1. Alice announces she wants to send $2 to Bob.
2. Everyone playing the lottery takes this transaction "Alice Gives $2 to Bob", adding a random number called a *nonce* (number used only once) at the end. This is to make sure that the string they're hashing is different from anyone else, helping them to find a winning lottery number.
3. If that number is smaller than the *Target Number* (we'll get to this in the next chapter), they win the lottery.
4. If the number they get is bigger than the Target Number, then they hash the same thing again, adding other random nonces: "Alice Gives $2 to Bob nonce=12345", then "Alice Gives $2 to Bob nonce=92435", then "Alice Gives $2 to Bob nonce=132849012348092134", and so on, until the resulting hash number is smaller than the Target Number.

It may take many, many tries to find a hash that is less than the Target Number. We can, in fact, control how often someone can win the lottery by controlling the probability of them finding a winning number. If there are 1000 possible hashes, and we set the Target Number to 100, then what percentage of hashes are under the Target?

This is basic math: 100 out of 1000 possible numbers or 100/1000 = 10% of hashes are less than the Target. So if you hash any string and your hash function produces 1000 different outputs, then you're expecting to get a hash that's under the Target of 100 about 10% of the time.

This is how the lottery works: we agree on a Target Number, then we all take the transactions that people have been telling us about, and hash them, adding a random nonce at the end. Once someone finds a hash that's under the Target, we announce it to everyone on the network:

Hey everyone:

- I took the transactions: "Alice Sends $2 to Bob, Charlotte Sends $5 to Alice".
- I added the nonce "32895".
- It came out to an output hash of 42 which is less than the Target of 100.
- Here's my Proof of Work: the transaction data, the nonce I used, and the hash that was produced based on those inputs.

It might have taken me billions of tries of hashing to get there, burning thousands of dollars of energy, but everyone else can immediately validate that I did in fact perform this work.

Since I gave them both the input data (transactions and nonce) and the expected output (the hash number), they can perform the same hash in one try and validate whether I gave them the right data.

We can think of hashing as rolling a giant die that produces numbers from zero to the number of atoms in the universe based on the input data which consists of transactions. Only hashes below the Target win the lottery and you have to show what data you used to produce the hash.

How does this tie into energy burning? Well, we already said the set of all possible hashes is actually a giant number that's about as big as the number of atoms in the universe. Now we can set the Target to be low enough so that only a tiny fraction of hashes are valid. This means that anyone who wants to find a valid hash will have to spend a huge amount of computation time, and therefore electricity, to find a hash number smaller than our Target.

The smaller the Target, the more tries it will take to find a number that works. The bigger the Target, the faster we can find a winning hash. If our chances of hitting the target are a million to 1, then by showing that we've hit it, we prove that we've run about a million calculations.

4
MINING

The process of playing the Proof of Work lottery to win access to write to the Bitcoin ledger is known popularly as *mining*. Here's how it works:

1. Anyone in the world who wants to participate, joins the Bitcoin network by connecting their computer and listening for transactions.
2. Alice announces her intent to send some coins to Bob. The computers on the network gossip with each other to spread this transaction to everyone on the network.
3. All the computers who want to participate in the lottery start hashing the transactions they heard about by appending random nonces to the transaction list, and running sha256 hash functions.
4. Roughly every ten minutes on average, some computer finds a hash number derived from those transactions that is less than the current Target Number and wins the lottery.
5. This computer announces the winning number they found, as well as the input (transactions and nonce) that they used to produce it. It might have taken them hours to get there, or a

few minutes. This information taken together (transactions, nonce, and the Proof of Work hash) is called a *block*.

6. Everyone else validates the block by checking that the transactions in the block together with the nonce do indeed hash to what was claimed, that the hash is indeed lower than the Target Number, and that the block does not contain any invalid transactions, and that the history within it does not conflict with prior blocks.
7. Everyone writes the block into their copy of the ledger, appending it into the existing chain of blocks, producing a *blockchain*.

That's it. We've produced our first block and our first entry into our ledgers.

You may have read the often repeated statement in the media that Bitcoin mining involves solving complex equations. You now understand that this is completely false. Rather than solving equations, the Bitcoin mining lottery is all about repeatedly rolling a giant virtual die to produce a hash within a certain target interval. It's simply a game of chance that forces the expenditure of a certain amount of electricity.

How are New Bitcoins Minted?

So far we discussed how Alice can send $2 to Bob. We're going to stop talking about dollars now, because Bitcoin doesn't know anything about dollars. What we do have are bitcoins themselves: digital units that represent value on the Bitcoin network.

To revisit our example, what's really happening is that Alice is sending 2 bitcoins to Bob by announcing that she's moving bitcoin that is registered under her "account" to Bob's. Someone then wins the Proof of Work lottery, and gets to write her transaction into the ledger.

But where did Alice get those 2 bitcoins to begin with? How did Bitcoin start, and how did anyone acquire coins before there were places to buy them for traditional fiat currency like the US dollar?

When Satoshi created Bitcoin, he could have created a database with him owning all 21 million coins and asked other people to buy them from him. However, there would be little reason for people to ascribe value to a system where one person owned all the wealth. He could have created a registry where people could sign up to win the chance to win some coins using an email address, but that would be susceptible to *sybil-attack* (impersonation) since generating millions of email addresses is nearly free.

It turns out the process of mining bitcoin, which is the process of playing the Proof of Work lottery and getting access rights to the ledger, is the very thing that produces new coins. When you find a valid block, by burning a large amount of energy and finding a number that wins the lottery, you get to write any transactions you've heard about into that block and therefore into the ledger. But you *also* get to write a very special additional transaction, called a *coinbase transaction* into the ledger. This transaction basically says: "12.5 Bitcoin were minted and given to Mary the Miner to compensate her for expending all that energy to mine this block."

This is how new bitcoins are minted into existence. This process allows absolutely anyone in the world to begin minting their own bitcoins without any central authority, and without identifying themselves, as long as they're willing to pay the cost of electricity required to play this lottery. This makes Bitcoin issuance resistant to a *sybil* attack. If you want coins, you're going to have to burn some energy and pay some money to mine them.

The Block Reward

The person who wins the lottery gets to give themselves some newly minted coins. Why is it 12.5 bitcoins and not 1000? Why can't she cheat the system and give herself any amount?

Bitcoin is a system of *distributed consensus*. That means everyone has to agree on what is valid. The way they do this is through running software on their computer that enforces a well known set of rules known as the Bitcoin consensus rules. Any block produced by a miner is validated through these rules. If it passes, everyone will write it into their ledger and accept it as truth. If not, the block is rejected.

Although the full list of consensus rules is rather complex, here are a few examples:

- A valid block may mint into existence a specific amount of Bitcoins as determined by the issuance schedule written into the software.
- Transactions must have correct signatures indicating that the people spending those coins have properly authorized those spends.
- There may not be any transactions that spend coins that have previously been spent in this block or any prior block.
- The data in the block must be no greater than a specific size.
- The Proof of Work hash of the block must be below the current Target Number, proving the statistical improbability of mining this block in any way other than having burned a certain amount of electricity.

If Mary mines a block and decides to give herself a little something extra, everyone else's computer will *reject* this block as *invalid*, because inside of the Bitcoin client software that everyone is running, there's a piece of code that says "the current Block Reward is exactly 12.5 bitcoin. If you see a block that grants someone more than that, do not accept it."

If Mary tries to cheat and produce an *invalid* block, the block won't get written to anyone's ledger, and instead she will just have wasted thousands of dollars of electricity producing something no one wants: a forgery. This gives Bitcoin an *unforgeable costliness*, a term coined by digital currency pioneer Nick Szabo in his essay *Shelling Out*. Intuitively, we know that if money was very easy to forge, it wouldn't be very useful as money. Bitcoin is actually impossible to counterfeit, as it is assayable by a simple mathematical check.

Satoshi mined the very first *genesis block* ever mined to generate the first bitcoins ever produced. The code is open source, meaning that anyone could take a look at how it works and validate that nothing fishy is going on under the hood. But even Satoshi had to run billions of computations and play the Proof of Work lottery in order to mine early blocks. He couldn't produce a forgery by faking the expenditure of the electricity required, even though he was the creator of the system.

Anyone joining the network after him was able to check his generated hash number against the initial Target and transaction data to verify that he had indeed hit a statistically rare Target by expending a certain amount of energy. Imagine being able to audit how the traditional fiat banking system mints money in this kind of precise and real-time manner!

The Halving

The mining process produces new Bitcoins. But Satoshi wanted a system that was not possible to *debase*. He didn't want the monetary supply to expand perpetually. Instead, he designed an emission schedule that started off quick and tapered off over time toward zero new coins per year.

In the beginning, the Block Reward was 50 bitcoins, so that's what Satoshi was rewarded for mining the first block, as did the other people who joined the network in the early days and mined the first blocks.

The Bitcoin code enforces a Block Reward Halving, which reduces the reward by half roughly every four years. This is based on the number of blocks mined, rather than the passage of time, but they are almost the same due to blocks being produced roughly every ten minutes.

The Block Reward in 2008 was 50, in 2012 was 25, in 2016 was 12.5. As of today, June 8, 2019 - there have been 579,856 blocks mined since the beginning of Bitcoin's history, and the reward is 12.5 bitcoin per block.

50,144 blocks from now, or approximately in late May, 2020, the reward will be lowered to 6.25 bitcoin per block, leading to an annual supply increase rate of approximately 1.8%. Twelve years later, following three more reward halvings, more than 99% of all Bitcoin will have been mined and less than 1 bitcoin will be produced per block. You can monitor the Block Reward Halving progress at bitcoinblockhalf.com.

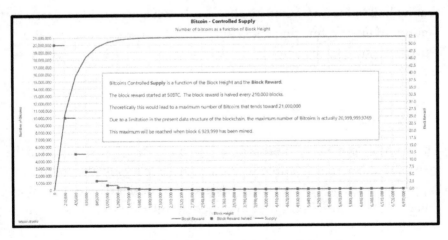

https://en.bitcoin.it/w/images/en/4/42/Controlled_supply-supply_over_block_height.png

Eventually, around the year 2140, the Block Reward will go away entirely, and miners will be incentivized only by fees paid by those performing the transactions.

These issuance and Block Reward numbers are enforced in the Bitcoin code—which, to reiterate, is completely open source and can be validated by anyone—so depending on how far along we are in Bitcoin's history, producing a block that doesn't follow these rules will get you rejected by everyone else who is checking the same rules written into their code.

Controlling the Issuance and Mining Interval

Mining requires computing hardware and electricity, so the more hardware and electricity you control, the more likely you are to find the winning number relative to other people. For example, if there are 100 equally powered computers on the network, and you control 10 of them, then you will find the winning block *approximately* 10% of the time. However, mining is a process based on chance and randomness, so it is possible that hours or even days can go by without you ever finding a block.

We know from the prior section that miners can't just grant themselves arbitrary block rewards, or they would get rejected by the other nodes. But what if they burn a whole bunch of energy to speed up mining blocks and get their hands on a whole lot of bitcoins, violating the design constraint that the issuance schedule should be known in advance?

Let's again go to the example of there being only 1000 possible hashes and our Target Number being 100. That means 10% of the time we will roll a number that's less than 100 and find a block.

Let's say it takes us 1 second to compute each hash. If each second we "roll our die" by hashing the current transactions and our random nonce, and 10% of the time we hit a number less than the Target, then we expect it will take us about 10 seconds on average to find a valid hash.

What happens if two computers are playing the lottery? They're hashing twice as fast, so we'll expect a valid hash to be found within 5 seconds. What if 10 computers are playing? Any one of them will find a winning hash approximately every second.

This creates a problem: if more people are mining, then blocks will be produced too quickly. This has two outcomes that we do not want:

1. It interferes with the idea of having a predetermined issuance schedule. We want a relatively consistent number of bitcoins per hour to be issued in order to make sure we issue all of them by the year 2140, and not any time ahead of that.
2. It creates networking problems: if blocks are mined so quickly that they don't have time to reach the entire network before the next one is mined, then we cannot come to consensus on a linear history of transactions, since multiple miners may include the same transaction in their blocks, leading to blocks being invalid because they contain transactions that were already spent in other blocks.

And if fewer people are mining, we create the opposite problem:

1. Bitcoins are being emitted too slowly, again interfering with the issuance schedule.
2. The system may become unusable as people wait hours, days, or longer, to get a transaction written to the ledger.

The total number of hashes per second performed by all the miners of the Bitcoin network is referred to as the *hash rate*.

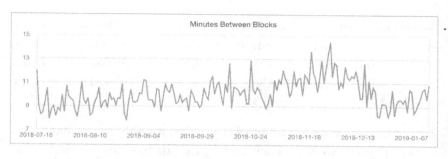

The time between blocks varies depending on hash rate coming and going as well as random chance.

Difficulty Adjustments: Agreeing on the Target

Since Bitcoin is a voluntary and permissionless system where people can participate as they please, with no one in charge, the number of miners at any one time will vary greatly. We need a way to keep block production steady, and not speed up and slow down every time new miners join or existing miners leave.

How can we make it harder to find valid hashes if more players join the lottery and easier if players leave the lottery, in order to keep the issuance and block times steady?

Recall that Bitcoin mining is a lottery where we are trying to produce a random number smaller than the Target:

We're trying to hit this little space. The number of possible outcomes is extremely large, so it will take us a very long time to get there through random rolls of the die.

Bitcoin solves this problem with a *mining difficulty adjustment*. Because everyone is running the same code, which enforces the same rules, and everyone has a copy of the entire history of blocks to this point, everyone can independently calculate how fast blocks are being produced.

Every time we produce 2016 blocks, which is roughly equivalent to two weeks of time[1], we look back and figure out how long it took us to produce those blocks, and then adjust our Target Number to speed up or slow down block production.

Everyone takes the last 2016 blocks and divides them by the time they took to produce to create an average. Did it come to more than ten minutes? We're going too slow. Did it come to less than ten minutes? We're going too fast.

Now we can make an adjustment to the Target Number so that it is raised or lowered proportionally to how much faster or slower we want to go based on the 10 minute interval which is written into the open source code.

We can raise the Target Number to a higher number, creating a larger space of valid hashes, giving miners a higher chance to find a winning hash, thus expending less energy per block found. This is called *lowering the difficulty*.

Increasing the target increases the space we need to hit, therefore making it more likely to hit in fewer tries, thus making it cheaper in energy burned.

Alternatively we can lower the Target Number so fewer hashes are valid, and miners have to spend more energy finding a valid block hash. This is called *raising the difficulty*.

This means that for any 2016 block period, we know exactly what the Target Number is. That lets us know the magic threshold under which the Proof of Work hash number has to fall for a winning lottery ticket for any block produced within that period.

The difficulty adjustment and Target calculation is possibly the key innovation of Bitcoin, allowing everyone to independently verify lottery numbers based on a Target that they can independently calculate in the same exact way as everyone else. This is what allows us to run a lottery without anyone telling us the winning combination.

The chart below shows the hash rate as a line, and the difficulty as bars over time. The difficulty looks like a staircase because it is adjusted in 2016 block increments. You can see that every time the hash rate rises above the difficulty, the difficulty steps up to catch up to the hash rate. When the hash rate falls, as it did between Oct-Dec of 2018, the difficulty steps down. The difficulty adjustment always lags behind whatever the hash rate does within the 2016-block (two week) difficulty period.

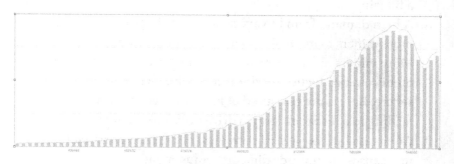

Hash Rate vs. Difficulty

Because there is a 2016 block lag for difficulty adjustment, it is possible for massive spikes up or down in hash rate to over or under produce

Bitcoin during that 2016 block period, slightly violating the issuance schedule.

Since adding hash rate typically means producing a large quantity of new hardware, spikes are relatively unusual and don't impact things too greatly. Any spiky effects are limited to the 2016 block window in which they occur, as the following difficulty adjustment gets us back to the ten minutes per block average.

Hash Rate and the Dollar Value of Bitcoin

Bitcoin automatically recomputes difficulty based on the total computing power of all lottery players, which are the miners expending energy through hashing. Here's where the real world starts to touch our digital world. The price of Bitcoin, the price of hardware and energy, and the difficulty Target Number create feedback loops:

1. Speculators buy bitcoin because they think it's going up, driving up the price to $X.
2. Miners spend up to $X of energy and hardware to try to mine a bitcoin.
3. A high demand from buyers causes a rise in price and drives more miners to mine bitcoin at a handsome profit.
4. More miners means more hash rate, and more energy spent on bitcoin production, and the network gets even more secure. Buyers are reassured of Bitcoin's security, sometimes leading to a feedback loop to drive price even higher.
5. After 2016 blocks pass, the presence of the newly arrived hash rate causes an upwards difficulty adjustment.
6. A larger difficulty means a lower Target Number—miners are finding blocks less often—causing at least some of them to spend more than $X in operating costs to mine a coin.
7. Some miners become unprofitable, spending more energy to

mine than they can earn by selling the bitcoin. They turn off their miners, and the total hash rate drops.
8. Another 2016 blocks pass. The difficulty is recomputed to become easier, since some miners went offline. The Target Number is raised.
9. A lower difficulty means that miners that were previously unprofitable can come back online and mine, or new miners can join the game.
10. Go to 1.

In a downward market, the cycle can go in the other direction, with users dumping coins, causing the price to go down, and miners to become unprofitable.

The difficulty adjustment algorithm ensures that there will always be an equilibrium between the price and the amount of hash rate mining on the network. Even if the price were to fall drastically and kick off half of the current hash rate, the subsequent difficulty adjustment would make mining profitable again at the new equilibrium price.

The nature of the difficulty adjustment pushes out inefficient miners in favor of ones operating on the cheapest possible energy with the lowest overall operational costs. Over time, this forces bitcoin miners to more remote parts of the world, using energy sources that are underutilized or completely untapped. A CoinShares report[2] from 2019 has estimated that approximately 75% of bitcoin mining is powered using renewable energy.

Over the last few years, the price has climbed very quickly, as has the total hash rate. The higher the hash rate, the harder it is to attack the network because in order to control what gets written to even just the next block, you'd need to have as much energy and hardware under your control as more than half of the entire network. Today, the energy expended by the network of Bitcoin miners is estimated as equivalent to that of a medium sized country.

Fees and The End of Block Rewards

If the Block Reward will eventually run out, how will we continue to incentivize miners to continue to burn energy to secure the ledger? Bitcoin's answer is transaction fees. Not only do they substitute the Block Reward over time, but they generally give miners incentive to include transactions in blocks so that they don't just mine empty ones for the reward.

Fees are determined by a free market system where users bid for scarce space in a block. Users who send transactions indicate how much in fees they are willing to pay to the miners, and miners may or may not include transactions that they see depending on the fees. When there are few transactions waiting to go into the next block, fees tend to be very low as there is no competition. As block space fills up, users are willing to pay higher fees for their transactions to be confirmed more quickly (within the next block). Those that don't want to pay can always set their fees low and wait longer to be mined at a later time when block space is more readily available.

In traditional financial systems, fees tend to be based on a percentage of the amount being transferred. In Bitcoin the value being transferred has no bearing on the fees. Instead, fees are proportional to the scarce resource they consume: block space. Fees are measured in satoshis per byte (8 bits) of space consumed. Thus, a transaction that sends a million bitcoins from one person to another could actually be cheaper than one that splits 1 bitcoin to 10 recipients because the latter requires more block space to represent.

In the past, there have been periods of time where Bitcoin was in very high demand, such as the massive bull run of late 2017. At this time, fees became extremely high. Since that time, a few new features have been implemented to reduce fee pressure on the network.

One of them is called Segregated Witness, which reorganized how block data is represented. Transactions that take advantage of this upgrade may use more than the original 1MB of block space through some clever tricks that are beyond the scope of this book.

The other relief to fees has come through batching: exchanges and other high volume players in the ecosystem started combining bitcoin transactions for multiple users into one transaction. Unlike a traditional payment in your bank or PayPal which is from one person to another, a Bitcoin transaction can combine a large number of inputs and produce a large number of outputs. Thus, an exchange that needs to send bitcoin for withdrawal to 100 people can do so in a single transaction. This is a much more efficient use of block space, turning what is ostensibly only a handful of bitcoin transactions per second into thousands of payments per second.

Segregated Witness and batching have already done a very good job in reducing demand for block space. Further improvements are in the pipeline that make use of the block space more efficient. Nonetheless, there will come a time when Bitcoin fees become high again as blocks get more and more full due to demand.

We've almost completed inventing all of Bitcoin:

1. Replaced a central bank with a distributed ledger.
2. Instituted a lottery system to select who writes to the ledger.
3. Forced lottery entrants to burn energy to buy tickets by hashing, and made it easy for everyone to verify winning tickets by checking the hash numbers produced by players against an independently calculated Target Number.
4. Told the lottery players that if they didn't play by the rules, we'd reject their blocks including their *coinbase transactions* so they wouldn't get paid when they won, thus creating an economic disincentive for cheating, and an economic incentive for playing by the rules.
5. Controlled the timing and Target selection for the lottery by letting everyone calculate for themselves what the Target

should be based on hardcoded rules and the history of the past 2016 blocks.
6. Enforced the issuance schedule using difficulty adjustments that adjust to increasing or decreasing hash rate.
7. Used open source code to ensure that everyone could verify for themselves that they were enforcing the same rules regarding transaction validity, block reward, and difficulty calculation.

No more central party. We have a fully distributed and decentralized system. We've almost got the entire picture. There remains one problem. When someone joins the network and asks for copies of the ledger, they may get different ledger histories from different nodes. How do we enforce a single, linear history, and how can we prevent miners from rewriting the past?

---

1. The adjustment period of 2016 blocks was chosen based on the desired ten minute block interval. 10 minutes x 2016 blocks is two weeks. The block interval was chosen by Satoshi arbitrarily to be big enough to have most nodes be able to sync to the latest block. The two week adjustment period was also picked somewhat arbitrarily, but designed to prevent the system from being gamed from overly quick changes in the hash rate.
2. Read more about the current state of mining at https://coinshares.co.uk/bitcoin-mining-cost-june-2019/

5

SECURING THE LEDGER

So far we talked about how we manage to keep copies and write to a distributed ledger without allowing for coercion or corruption, using a lottery system and validation by consensus.

But what happens when a lottery winner wants to get malicious? Can a miner change historical entries in the ledger? Can our malicious actors Eve, Dave, and Farrah collude in order to rewrite history or change account balances and give themselves extra coins?

Enter the *blockchain*. A marketing term that has permeated much of the tech sector, the blockchain is nothing more than the idea that Bitcoin *blocks* are *chained* together to provide links from one set of transactions to the next. This creates a linear history of coin minting and spending from Satoshi's *genesis block* in 2009 through today.

We lied a little in the prior chapter to keep things simple. When you mine by playing the Proof of Work lottery, the transactions in line for the next block plus a random nonce aren't the only thing being hashed together. You're also adding in the hash of the block that came before yours, thereby linking your block to the prior block.

Recall that the output of a hash function is unpredictable and dependent on all the data input into it. We've now modified our block hashes to include three different inputs:

1. The transactions we want to commit to the ledger.
2. A random nonce.
3. The hash of the prior block that we're using as the basis of our ledger's history.

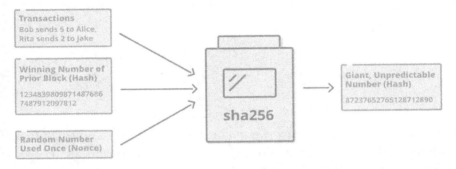

The three inputs used to build a hash number for the lottery now include the prior winning hash, making a link from one block to the next.

This enables us to build a historical record of every block back to the very first genesis block mined by Satoshi. When we write a new block into the chain, we have to validate that this block does not contain any transactions that spend bitcoins that were already spent in prior blocks.

If any of the hash inputs change, the output hash changes in an unpredictable and drastic way. If you tamper with data in any historical block, you will change its hash. But because that hash was used as input to subsequent blocks, you will end up also changing the hashes of those blocks. The hash from the latest block in the chain, being connected to all the prior hashes, acts as a fingerprint of the entire history of the chain up to that point!

You can't cheat Proof of Work since everyone knows how much energy burn has to go into every block based on the Target Number required for that block. If anyone were to try to change an older block in the chain, they would have to recompute the Proof of Work hash of the block they're tampering with and every single block that comes afterwards. Not only is the blockchain tamper evident, but it is *extremely costly* to tamper with.

Effectively, every new block that is mined adds to the security of the blocks that came before it, as it adds to the amount of electricity required to recompute the Proof of Work hashes for the chain to that point. A transaction in a block that is buried under 6 subsequent blocks is considered final by most merchants today. It would take a tremendous amount of energy to rehash the last six blocks at today's total hash rate. One that's 100 blocks deep? Forget about it.

When you download a copy of the blockchain, every transaction in each block is fully transparent, and you can check the Proof of Work hashes yourself to ensure that nothing was altered by the person who sent you the ledger.

When Blocks Collide

There is one missing piece of the consensus system: how can we force everyone onto the same linear history of transactions if miners simultaneously mine two blocks and send them out to everyone?

Imagine we are now running a worldwide network. People across the world, from the U.S. to China are connected to this global network and they're all playing the Proof of Work mining lottery.

Someone in Chicago finds a valid block. They announce it to the network, and all the computers across America start picking it up. Meanwhile, someone in Shanghai also finds a block within a few seconds of the Chicago block. Their neighbors still haven't heard about the American block, so they hear about the Chinese block first.

Both of these blocks contain a transaction of 1 bitcoin from Alice to

Bob. But immediately after receiving that bitcoin, Bob sends it to Charlie. Due to timing differences, the American block reflects this transaction, and Bob has a final balance of zero. However, the Chinese mined their block before seeing Bob's spend to Charlie. The Chinese block shows Bob's balance at 1 bitcoin.

The network is divided on which blockchain is the correct copy of the ledger, since both contain valid transactions that are linked to the history in all the blocks that came before them. Both contain a valid amount of Proof of Work. This is called a *chain split*. You can't rely on any central party to tell you which one wins. What do you do?

Bitcoin provides for a simple solution here: let's just wait and see. Miners are free to choose which block they want to use as their base for subsequent mining. The Americans will be mining to link to the block they first heard about, and the Chinese will be mining on top of their own block.

In the next roughly ten minute period, another block will be mined. In the Bitcoin code, there is a rule that says whomever has expended the most total energy for all of the blocks in their chain wins. This key rule of Bitcoin that asks us to sum up the total Work in a chain and favor the heaviest cumulative Proof of Work chain is sometimes called Nakamoto Consensus, in honor of Satoshi.

Let's say the Chinese mine the next block. Their chain is now one block ahead of the American one and contains more total Proof of Work. When they broadcast this finding, the American nodes will recognize that the Chinese nodes have produced a heavier cumulative Proof of Work chain, and reorganize (or *reorg*). That means they will throw away the one block they mined in favor of the two Chinese ones.

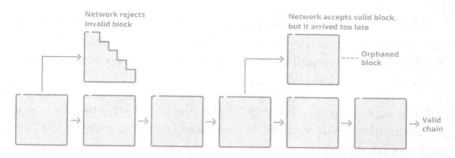

A chain split is a natural process that occurs when miners find a block at the same time. The chain that becomes heavier by total proof of work is valid, and the other block becomes orphaned.

The American block is now called an *orphan*. Since it was rejected, the miner who mined it didn't get his reward, and none of the transactions in that block are committed to the ledger. The rejected transactions are not lost, however. Some of them may have made it into the competing Chinese block, and any that didn't will eventually be written into a future block.

Miners store all transactions they hear about in a special place on their computer called the *mempool*. Any transactions from a rejected block are put back into the mempool. They are then mined by someone in the future as long as they don't conflict with the new ledger history produced by the latest block.

You may notice that even though we've referred to nodes as American and Chinese, in reality the nodes don't know anything about each other's identity or geographic location. The only proof of validity they need is that someone has the heaviest cumulative Proof of Work chain, and that the transactions in the chain are themselves all valid (not double-spends, etc).

These kinds of chain splits are normal and happen from time to time in Bitcoin. They are usually resolved within the next block. Improvements in block propagation technology and networking connectivity between miners make this problem less of an issue over time. Today and likely for the foreseeable future, Bitcoin has a hardcoded limit on the amount of data allowed into a block. Part of the reason Bitcoin produces relatively small blocks roughly ten minutes apart is to ensure that orphans are extremely rare.

Mining is probabilistic. Sometimes the blocks are ten minutes apart, and other times just seconds. If we produced blocks every second or had very large blocks, we would have a high probability that American and Chinese blocks would conflict because they're far apart geographically and take longer to reach each other. If orphans happen too often, then the blockchain would unravel. There would be orphans upon orphans and nodes would not have time to agree on the latest block before the next block was mined.

It is important to keep blocks small to increase the chance that the entire network can receive the latest block before mining the next one. The other, and perhaps more important reason, is to keep the hardware requirements for running a node relatively low to encourage more nodes and more decentralized mining in the system over time. Large blocks would encourage miners to colocate in data centers and geographic regions in order to avoid orphaned blocks, which negatively impact their profitability.

The One True Chain

Let's go back to our example from Chapter 3 where Henry joins the Bitcoin network for the first time.

Henry's node will connect to a few other nodes on the network, and ask them about nodes they know, and then connect to some of those nodes as well. This is called node discovery.

Some of these nodes will be outright evil and will feed him a false copy of the ledger, with incorrect signatures for transactions, or forged and improperly minted bitcoins that do not have valid Proof of Work hashes. Those copies will be rejected outright, and those nodes will be instantly banned from further connecting to Henry's node[1].

Other nodes he connects to will be honest, but will have conflicting versions of the truth. For example, some of them may have gotten knocked offline and be a block or two behind. If he downloads multiple copies of the blockchain, all of which are equally valid, the software in his node will use Nakamoto Consensus. Measuring the total cumulative Proof of Work, whichever chain is the heaviest will be considered the One True Chain.

Nodes constantly communicate with each other to make sure they have the latest blocks. Since all nodes follow the heaviest chain rule, there is consensus on what the true state of the ledger is. Henry does not have to rely on majority vote, which would be easy to cheat by making the majority of nodes evil.

Even if Henry connects to dozens of out of date or malicious nodes, and one correct node, his Bitcoin software will know the one correct copy because it will contain the greatest amount of Proof of Work and consist of valid transactions all the way back to the genesis block. The importance of this cannot be understated. Henry needs not to rely on trusting anyone; his node will perform all the validations to ensure the blockchain he is looking at is the One True Chain.

It is extremely difficult, therefore, for malicious hackers to give a node a false copy of the blockchain. To do so would require severing that node's connection to any other honest nodes and connecting it only to nodes controlled by the attackers.

Reversibility of Transactions

Two competing chains are usually produced by chance and are quickly resolved. However, someone that wants to attack the network can take advantage of Nakamoto Consensus by controlling more than 50% of the total hash rate. They can then produce the heaviest cumulative Proof of Work chain containing transactions of their choosing, as long as they're willing to burn enough energy to do so. When they broadcast this chain, other nodes would accept it as the One True Chain. This is called a *51% attack* because it requires controlling more than half of the hash rate.

It's important to understand that there is no actual transaction finality in Bitcoin, since 51% attacks or even chance orphaning of blocks are always theoretically possible. Because of this, recipients of transactions typically wait for several blocks to be mined on top of a transaction in order to consider it set in stone. At that point, the amount of energy required to reverse the transaction is so expensive that it isn't likely going to happen.

Blocks mined on top of a block containing a transaction of interest to you are often called *confirmations*. So when you hear that a Bitcoin transaction has six confirmations, that means six blocks have been mined on top of it. If you're selling a digital book that has marginal cost to you as a merchant, you might only want 1 confirmation, or even zero confirmations, delivering the download link as soon as you see the transaction broadcast on the network. If you're selling a house, maybe you want to wait for twelve confirmations, or roughly two hours of mining. The longer you wait, the more Proof of Work is piled on top of the block that contains your transaction, and the more real world costly it becomes to reverse the transaction. Today, most people accept 6 confirmations as proof of payment.

If the hash rate of Bitcoin were to fall significantly, meaning that less energy was securing each block, one could always increase the number of confirmations they would require for final settlement. Although the non-finality of transactions may seem disconcerting at first, it's important to keep in mind that credit card transactions can typically be reversed 120 days after they are made.

On the other hand, Bitcoin transactions are nearly irreversible only a few blocks in. From this standpoint, the reversibility and finality of

Bitcoin transactions is actually a vast improvement to that of most traditional payment networks, at least from the merchant's perspective.

Today's estimates show that if you had the energy of the entire Bitcoin network at your disposal—a lofty proposition indeed, as you would have to harness a country-sized amount of energy and every specialized bit of Bitcoin hardware out there—it would still take you more than a year to rewrite the entire history of the chain. You can explore this data at http://bitcoin.sipa.be.

---

1. This excellent essay dives deep into how bitcoin deals with invalid blocks: https://hackernoon.com/bitcoin-miners-beware-invalid-blocks-need-not-apply-51c293ee278b

6

FORKS AND 51% ATTACKS

In the beginning, Satoshi mined the first bitcoins using his computer's central processing unit (CPU). Since the initial mining difficulty in the system was set low, it was relatively inexpensive for his computer to generate these coins.

Over time, people started tweaking the mining software to make it more and more efficient. Eventually, they wrote software that started taking advantage of specialized graphics processing units (GPUs) which are usually used for gaming.

With GPUs, mining became an order of magnitude more efficient than CPU mining. The difficulty quickly adjusted upward to match all the new hash rate that flooded the system using GPUs. At this point, anyone mining on a CPU became unprofitable and had to turn off their miner.

After the advent of GPU mining, the efficiency of mining was tweaked even more through the production of Application Specific Integrated Circuits, or *ASICs*. These are hardware computer chips that do only one thing: the bitcoin sha256 function and nothing else. Being specialized to this particular algorithm, ASICs were an order of magnitude more efficient than GPUs for mining, and the difficulty adjusted upward, quickly making GPUs unprofitable, just like GPUs had done to CPUs. Every few years, a new generation of ASIC devices would put earlier versions out of business with large efficiency improvements.

The first few miners on the network expended only a few pennies of electricity in order to produce their bitcoins. As the price of bitcoin rose, and more and more miners joined, the difficulty went up, and it became more and more expensive to generate bitcoins. Today, the price hovers close to $8000 per coin, and people burn thousands of dollars of electricity per bitcoin created.

Mining Pools

One issue with bitcoin mining is that it is nondeterministic, like rolling a die. That means you could end up spending a lot of money on electricity yet never find a valid block.

In 2010, an innovation called a *mining pool* emerged to address the problem of miners burning electricity without receiving reward. A mining pool is a shared risk pool, similar to how insurance works.

All the miners contribute to mining for the pool, thus creating the appearance of one large miner. If anyone in the pool finds a valid block, the reward for the block is proportionally split amongst all the miners based on the hash rate they contributed. This allows even small mining operations such as individuals to receive reward for the small amount of hash rate they contribute. For providing this coordination service, the pool takes a cut of the rewards.

Mining pools caused some effect of centralization—users flocked to bigger pools. However, it is important to remember that users are mining for pools and that pools do not own all the hash rate they represent. Users can and do switch mining pools over time.

In fact, there is historic precedent for individual miners leaving a pool that became too powerful. In 2014, Ghash.io had close to half of the total mining power. Miners saw it creeping toward being too centralized and left for other pools voluntarily.

While relatively centralized mining pools are the reality today, there are constant improvements to mining technology including a proposal called BetterHash, which lets individual miners be more in control of what they're mining and reduce reliance on coordination from pools.

51% Attacks

Mining pool centralization leads to the worry that a few of the top pools could collude to 51% attack the network. Today, the top 5 identifiable pools together have more than 50% of the total mining hash rate. Let's examine how such an attack is performed and what dangers it carries.

When you own just over 50% of the hash rate, you can dominate the writes into the ledger because you can produce a heavier chain than the others over time. Remember that Nakamoto Consensus says that nodes must accept the heaviest cumulative Proof of Work chain that they hear about.

Here's an example of how a very simple 51% attack is carried out:

1. Let's say the network as a whole is mining bitcoin at 1000 hashes/second.
2. You buy up a bunch of mining hardware and electricity to produce 2000 hashes/second. You now have 66% of the total hash rate (2000 of 3000 hashes per second).
3. You start mining a chain that contains only empty blocks.
4. Two weeks from now, you broadcast your chain of empty blocks. Because you are mining approximately twice as fast as the honest miners, your chain will be twice as heavy by cumulative Proof of Work. Broadcasting to all the existing

nodes will cause them to reorg and lose the last two weeks of history.

Besides mining empty blocks, which makes the chain unusable, you can also perform a double spend attack:

1. Send some bitcoin to an exchange.
2. Exchange it to USD and withdraw the USD.
3. At some later date, broadcast a chain you mined secretly which does not contain the send to the exchange.
4. You've rewritten history and now have both the original bitcoins and the USD.

The energy consumption of Bitcoin's hash rate today is roughly equivalent to that of a decent sized country. Acquiring enough hardware and electricity to perform such an attack is extremely expensive. Estimates show that it would cost you roughly $700k per hour to perform a 51% attack today, and this cost continues to rise. This estimate also doesn't take into account the reaction of the honest miners to such an attack, which would likely make it even more expensive. You can explore the cost to attack Bitcoin and other cryptocurrencies at https://www.crypto51.app.

It's also very difficult to get away with a double-spend attack of this proportion without leaving footprints behind that could be used to figure out who you are. After all, you would be burning the energy of a medium sized country and buying up millions of dollars in hardware, as well as sending millions of dollars to exchanges in order to execute the attack.

But let's say some malicious entity with unlimited funding, such as a government, did decide to do this and was able to sustain this attack beyond the level of a nuisance. The network could then theoretically adapt by changing to a different Proof of Work function (not sha256). This would render all the Bitcoin mining hardware used by the attacker useless, as it is only specialized for doing sha256 hashing. However, changing Proof of Work is a nuclear option that would immediately put out of business all the honest miners as well. Nonetheless, the network would survive and arise from the ashes.

In addition to the infeasibility of the attack, having the majority of the hash rate does not entitle you to the two things that matter most:

1. You can't create coins out of thin air that violate the issuance schedule. This violates the block reward consensus rule and your blocks would be rejected, even if they had enough Proof of Work.
2. You can't spend coins that aren't yours. You wouldn't be able to provide a valid digital signature, which violates the rules.

The nodes that accept Bitcoin as payment would keep the network honest even in the face of a dishonest majority of miners by simply enforcing the rules of Bitcoin. As such, a 51% attack is more of a nuisance than a security concern. Most likely, the worst case scenario here is a state actor with deep pockets trying to make Bitcoin unusable. However, such an attack cannot be sustained forever. When Bitcoin recovers from an attack like that, it would only further prove its resilience and become an even bigger problem for those who would attack it.

Although to this day Bitcoin has never been successfully 51% attacked, the attack has been performed on other blockchains that have very little hash rate securing them. In these cases, exchanges were victims of double-spend attacks and lost money on low hash rate coins they likely shouldn't have listed in the first place.

7
ACCOUNTS WITHOUT IDENTITY

We have built a distributed ledger with no central authority, a mining lottery system for selecting who writes to it, a system for rewarding good miners and punishing misbehaving ones, a way to adjust mining difficulty to ensure a consistent issuance schedule and reduce conflicts, and a system for checking the validity of the chain by looking at the cumulative proof of work and transaction history.

Now let's deal with identity. In a traditional banking system, you send money by identifying yourself to the bank. You present an ID and pin code at the ATM, or type a username and password into an app. The bank ensures that no two entities share an identity.

Since we now have no central party to keep track of identities, how can we open accounts in our new Bitcoin based financial system? How can we address Satoshi's goal of removing identity from financial transactions, to avoid identity theft and trusting central parties with our information? How can we ensure that when Alice announces she wants to pay Bob, that it's really her and that she has authority to move those funds?

Generating a "Bitcoin Account"

We can't rely on a central middleman like a bank to keep a record of all accounts. What if we let everyone register their own username and password? A bank would normally check that a username isn't already in use, but that's not possible here, since we have no central actor handing out identities. We need something bigger, stronger, and more unique than a username and password. This technique should be familiar from prior chapters. We once again need a giant random number.

Just like we made it possible for everyone to buy lottery tickets by generating large random numbers, we can use the same trick for generating accounts. To create a "Bitcoin Account," also known as an *address*, we will first generate a pair of 256 bit numbers that are mathematically linked, known as a *public/private key pair*. Remember, a 256 bit number is roughly as large as the number of atoms in the universe, so two people accidentally generating the same key pair is next to impossible. We'll give out our address to anyone who wants to send us coins. We'll use the private key to spend the coins. Here's how it works.

Encryption is a method for taking some data and obscuring it, so that only someone who has the key can read the original message by decrypting it. As kids, some of us played with basic encoder/decoder toys that used a key to change a message into gibberish and then back again. This kind of encryption is called symmetric, using only one key. The public/private key pair system is *asymmetric* because you can encrypt with one key, and decrypt with the other.

You are welcome to share your public key with the entire world. People who want to send you messages can encrypt them with your public key. Because only you have the private key, you are the only one who can decrypt them.

Let's take a look at how Alice sends coins to Bob. To receive a transaction, Bob generates a key pair, and keeps his private key secret. He

Inventing Bitcoin

produces an *address*, a large number based on a hash of his public key. Bob then shares this address number with Alice.

You can think of the address as a mailbox. Instead of letters, Alice can drop coins into this mailbox. But only Bob has the private key that opens the mailbox in order to spend the coins.

When you move money in a bank, you give them your username and password. When you write checks, you sign your name to authenticate that it's you writing the check. When you move bitcoins, you provide proof that you own the key to the address that holds the coins.

Alice needs to prove that she has the private key to her public key mailbox, but she doesn't want to to expose her private key to hackers, or they would be able to steal it and spend from her mailbox.

Alice's proof of key ownership is called a *digital signature*. Alice constructs a transaction, which is essentially a piece of data that looks something like this:

```
Address  12345  containing  2.5  bitcoins  is
sending  2 bitcoins  to address  56789 and  0.5
bitcoins back to address 12345
```

In reality, the address numbers are giant 160-bit numbers. She then encrypts the same transaction with her private key, creating a *digital signature*.

When she publishes her transaction to other nodes on the network, she reveals the public key of the mailbox she's sending from, and the private-key encrypted signature. Alice announces the following:

- I am sending coins from address 12345
- Here is the public key for address 12345, and you can see that it is in fact the public key by hashing the public key and seeing that you get the address.

- Here is a signature which I've encrypted with the private key corresponding to this address. You can use the public key to decrypt it and verify that it is identical to the transaction data I'm sending.

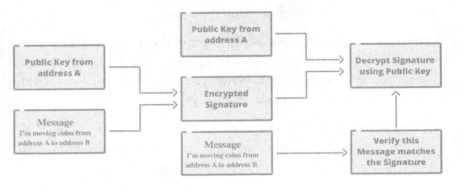

The transaction that moves coins is encrypted using the private key to create a digital signature. It is decrypted using the public key, which everyone knows.

Since everyone now has Alice's public key for her mailbox address, they can easily decrypt the digital signature. By virtue of being able to correctly decrypt the signature using the public key for the address, everyone knows that Alice must have used the private key to that address to create the signature. Otherwise, their decryption would have failed since the public key can only decrypt messages encrypted with the private key. But importantly, they have not actually seen her private key, but rather only proof that she was able to use it for encrypting her signature.

Unlike a signature on a check or your bank password, your digital signature is specific to the unique transactional data that you are signing. Thus it can't be stolen and reused on a different transaction. Every transaction gets a different signature, even if it's being sent from the same public address, with the same private key, since any new data changes the signature hash.

Can You Guess a Private Key?

Let's figure out the odds of guessing a private key, which would give you the ability to move the coins at the corresponding public address. Remember, a key is made up of 256 bits. Each bit has only two values (one or zero). That means you can visualize each bit like a coin toss.

If we had a 1-bit private key, it's like tossing a single coin. Heads or tails, one or zero? You have a one in two chance of guessing right.

Quick basic stats review: the probability of multiple events occurring is calculated by multiplying together each event's individual probability. If a coin toss has a 1/2 chance of landing heads, then the chance of two coin tosses in a row landing heads is 1/2 x 1/2 = 1/4 or 1 in 4.

If you were to guess the outcome of 8 coin tosses in a row that would be 2^8, or a one in 256 chance.

A license plate has 6 letters and numbers. There are 26 letters and 10 numbers, so a total of 36 characters. Since there are six of them, the number of possible license plates = 36^6, so your odds of guessing mine are one in two billion[1].

A credit card is sixteen digits. Each digit can have 10 values, and there are 16 of them so your odds of guessing my credit card are one in 10^{16}, which is one in 10,000,000,000,000,000 or roughly one in ten quadrillion.

There are about 10^{50} atoms on earth. If I'm thinking of one at random, your chances of guessing it are about

> One in 1,000,000,000,000,000,000,000,000,000,000,
> 000,000,000,000,000,000,000,000.

A private key has 256 bits, which is 2^{256} or about 10^{77}. Guessing the entire key would be similar to guessing a specific atom from the entire universe, or winning the Powerball Lottery 9 times in a row:

One chance in 115,792,089,237,316,195,423,570,985, 008,687,907,853,269,984,665,640,564,039,457,584,007,913,129,639,936

But what if you had a super powerful computer to do the guessing? I can't do this subject justice more than the Reddit post at https://bit.ly/2Dbw9Qd, which I recommend reading in its entirety. While it gets technical, the final paragraph gives you a good idea of what it would take to list all possible 256-bit keys:

> "So, if you could use the entire planet as a hard drive, storing 1 byte per atom, using stars as fuel, and cycling through 1 trillion keys per second, you'd need 37 octillion Earths to store it, and 237 billion suns to power the device capable of doing it, all of which would take you 3.6717 octodecillion years."
>
> — u/PSBlake on r/Bitcoin

Basically, it's impossible for you to guess someone's private key. Not only that, but the number of possible Bitcoin addresses is so large, that Bitcoin best practices actually call for generating a new address with a new private key for every transaction you make. So instead of having one bank account, you might have thousands or even millions of Bitcoin accounts, one for every transaction you've ever received.

It may be disconcerting that your Bitcoin account is secured only by chance, but hopefully the explanation above gives you an idea that this is vastly more secure than the password to your bank account, stored on a centralized server, available to hackers.

Tracking Balances

It's time to correct one final white lie we've repeated in prior chapters. There aren't actually any balances kept in the ledger. Instead, Bitcoin uses a model called UTXO: Unspent Transaction Outputs. A transaction output is just the word for coins you've received in a prior transaction, whether they came from someone sending them to you, or from mining them in a *coinbase transaction*.

Unlike metal coins that may come in specific denominations like ten cents, twenty five cents, and so on, bitcoins are divisible into 100,000,000 units called satoshis. Therefore, depending on what denominations you've received to your addresses, you may need to combine coins from multiple addresses, or split apart a larger UTXO to turn it into smaller ones for sending to someone else. Think of it like sending a bunch of coins into a machine that melts them down and mints new coins of any denomination you want. Wallets, discussed later in this chapter, generally manage all this for you behind the scenes so that you simply specify the amount you want to send.

Let's say Alice has an address that contains 1 bitcoin. She wants to send 0.3 bitcoins to Bob. She generates a transaction that shows her address with a 1 bitcoin UTXO as an input and two outputs: a new bitcoin UTXO worth 0.3 to Bob's address, and a new bitcoin UTXO worth 0.7 back to her own address as change. The change can go to her original sending address, or for better privacy, she can send it to a new address that she generates on the fly.

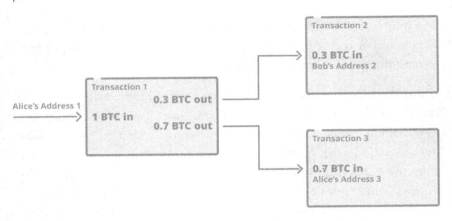

If you don't have a UTXO in the exact amount that you want to send, then one will be split to create change. You could also combine multiple UTXOs to create a new larger one.

There's no way on the chain to tell who controls which address. For that, you'd need to know the corresponding private keys and tie them to real world identities. The UTXO model encourages a very nice privacy mechanism through sending change to a new address every time coins are moved. Thus, a person may own hundreds or thousands of addresses if they've sent or received coins many times. Wallet software manages all of this for us, so we don't have to worry about the details.

Thus, to check the "balance" of a particular address, we actually have to add up all the UTXOs that have this address as an output. The total set of current UTXOs in Bitcoin grows when people send from one address to many, and shrinks when people perform *consolidation* transactions where coins from many addresses are spent to one address.

The UTXO model allows for easy and efficient validation of double spends, since any particular UTXO can only be spent once. We do not need to know the entire history of spends from a particular account.

We can also create and destroy any number of UTXOs at once, creating complex transactions that mix different inputs and outputs.

This allows for the idea of CoinJoin[2] where multiple parties participate in a single Bitcoin transaction that mixes any number of inputs to produce any number of outputs, thus obscuring the history of the UTXOs. The popularity of such techniques is rising and is important for privacy and *fungibility*, which is a term that says that any one bitcoin is equivalent to any other bitcoin. That way, if some bitcoins end up in the hands of unsavory parties, they aren't tainted for eternity just because they were used for something nefarious one time.

Wallets

Generating an account is nothing more than generating a random 256 bit key pair. We can create thousands or millions of accounts, so we need a way to track them. In Bitcoin, the word *wallet* is used to refer to any kind of device that tracks your keys. It could be as simple as a piece of paper or as complex as a piece of hardware.

The original Bitcoin code published by Satoshi came with a software wallet. This wallet would generate your addresses for you, store your keys, and select UTXOs for you to spend so that you could easily send bitcoins of any denomination.

Unlike your bank's wallet, which is typically in the form of a mobile or web application produced by your bank, Bitcoin is a completely open system. Thus there are dozens of wallets, most of which are free, many of which are also open source, as well as a half dozen hardware wallet implementations with more coming. Anyone with knowledge of computer programming can build their own wallet or read the code of an open source wallet to ensure nothing fishy is going on.

Since your private key is the only thing you need to spend your coins, you must guard it very closely. If someone steals your credit card, you can call up the company and file a fraud complaint and try to get your money back. In Bitcoin, there is no intermediary. If someone has your private key, they control your coins, and there's no one you can call.

Private keys are also susceptible to loss. If you store your wallet on your computer and the computer is stolen or catches fire, you have a problem. If you follow Bitcoin best practices in generating a new address every time you receive payments, securely storing and backing up these private keys becomes quickly burdensome.

Over time, the Bitcoin ecosystem has evolved a number of solutions to this problem. In 2012, BIP32 (Bitcoin Improvement Proposal, a mechanism for people to spread ideas on how to improve Bitcoin) was proposed to create Hierarchical Deterministic Wallets. The idea behind this is that using only a single random number called a *seed*, we can continuously generate many key pairs representing bitcoin addresses and private keys for them.

Nowadays, if you use any of the commonly available software or hardware wallets, they will automatically generate new keys for you for every transaction, allowing you to back up only a single master key.

In 2013, BIP39 came along to make key backup even easier. Instead of using a random number, keys would be generated from a random set of human readable words instead. Here's an example seed:

```
witch collapse practice feed shame open
despair creek road again ice least
```

With this method, backing up keys became very easy: you could write the seed on a piece of paper and put it into a safety deposit box. You could even memorize the phrase and walk out of a failing economic regime like Venezuela with nothing on your person, no one being the wiser that you're carrying your wealth in your head.

Furthermore, a Bitcoin address can require more than one private key to access. Multisignature or *multisig* addresses may employ a large variety of security schemes. For example, two people can share an account using 1-of-2 multisig, where either party can sign for transactions and spend coins.

A 2-of-2 multisig that requires both parties to supply keys to spend can be used to prevent any single person from gaining control of an account, for example between business partners.

You can make a simple escrow system using a 2-of-3 multisig. The buyer gets one key, the seller gets another key, and a third key is given to an arbitrator. If buyer and seller agree, they can unlock the funds together. In the case of a dispute, the arbitrator can act in concert with one of the parties to unlock the funds.

You can use a 3-of-5 multisig scheme to protect yourself from loss of keys by allowing yourself to lose up to 2 of the 5 keys and still being able to unlock the account. You can store two of the keys in different places, two with different trusted friends that don't know each other, and one with a specialized custodian service like BitGo which co-signs your transactions, making your Bitcoin very difficult to steal while protecting yourself from loss of keys.

You can go even further and make addresses that are unlocked by rather complex conditions using programming constructs such as conditional statements ("if this, then that"). You could even lock up coins in an address that is only accessible 10 years from now, and not even you as the creator of such an address can change your mind and alter the code to spend those coins ahead of time.

More and more semi-custodial solutions are arising from companies such as Casa and Unchained Capital, which help you store keys in a secure way. Unlike a bank, which can freeze your account, these partial custody solutions act as a backup or trusted co-signer, but cannot themselves take your funds without your keys. Wallet software is constantly evolving because it doesn't require anyone's permission to do so, unlike your bank's app. Therefore we're seeing more new entrants and more innovation all the time.

This is profound and world-changing. Never before has it been possible to carry your wealth in a way completely safe from seizure or theft.

---

1. The inspiration for this section came from an excellent Medium post which details the probabilities of a variety of events. I recommend reading the full post for context: https://medium.com/@kerbleski/a-dance-with-infinity-980bd8e9a781
2. https://en.bitcoin.it/wiki/CoinJoin

8

WHO MAKES THE RULES?

We've now got a functional distributed system for keeping track of and transferring value. Let's review what we've built so far:

1. A distributed ledger, a copy of which is kept by every participant.
2. A lottery system based on Proof of Work and difficulty adjustments to keep the network secure from tampering and the issuance schedule consistent.
3. A consensus system that ensures that every participant can validate the entire history of the blockchain for themselves using an open source piece of software called the Bitcoin client.
4. An identity system using digital signatures that allows for the arbitrary creation of account-like mailboxes that can receive coins without a central authority.

Now it's time to tackle one of the most interesting and counterintuitive things about Bitcoin. Where do its rules come from, how are they enforced, and how can they change over time?

The Bitcoin Software

Throughout the prior chapters, we assumed that everyone on the network is validating the same rules: they are rejecting double-spends, ensuring that every block contains the appropriate amount of Proof of Work, that each block points to the prior block at the tip of the current blockchain, and that each transaction in each block is correctly signed for by the owner of its address, amongst a whole bunch of other things that people have agreed to over time.

We also said Bitcoin is an open source piece of software. Open source means anyone can read its code, and also that anyone can update their own copy with whatever code they want. How do changes make it into Bitcoin?

Bitcoin is a *protocol*. In computer software, this term refers to a set of rules that the software follows. However, as long as you follow the set of rules that everyone else is following, you are free to modify your software as you wish. When we say that people "run Bitcoin nodes," what we really mean is they run software that speaks the Bitcoin protocol. This software can communicate with other Bitcoin nodes, transmit transactions and blocks to them, discover other nodes to peer with, and so on.

The actual details of how they implement the Bitcoin protocol is up to any individual's choice. There are many implementations of the Bitcoin protocol. The most popular of these is called Bitcoin Core, and is the extension of the work first released by Satoshi Nakamoto.

There are other implementations as well, written in other computer languages and maintained by different people. Because consensus in Bitcoin is critical, meaning all nodes must agree on which blocks are or are not valid, the vast majority of nodes run the same Bitcoin Core software in order to avoid any incidental bugs that may cause some nodes to disagree on what is valid. In fact, there is no fully complete written specification of the Bitcoin protocol, so the best bet for implementing new Bitcoin client software is to read the original code and make sure you don't deviate from what it does, even if it has bugs.

Who Makes the Rules?

The rules that make up Bitcoin are encoded into the Bitcoin Core client. But who decides these rules? Why do we say that Bitcoin is scarce if someone can come in and make a modification to the software that changes the 21 million bitcoin limit to 42 million?

Being a distributed system, all the nodes must agree to the rules. If you're a miner and you decide to change your software to grant yourself twice as much reward as you're allowed by the current Block Reward setting, then when you mine your block, every other node in the network will reject your block. Making a change to the rules is extremely hard because there are thousands of nodes distributed across the world, each enforcing the rules of Bitcoin.

Bitcoin's governance model is counterintuitive, especially to those of us living in a western democracy. We are used to governance by voting—the majority of people can decide to do something, pass a law, and impose their will on the minority. But Bitcoin's system of governance is much closer to anarchy than democracy.

Each person who accepts Bitcoin payments decides for themselves what they consider to be Bitcoin. If someone runs software that says there are 21 million bitcoins, and you try to send them bitcoins produced by your rogue software that defies this limit, your coins will appear as counterfeit to them and be rejected.

Let's take a look at the actors in the Bitcoin world that act as checks and balances on each other.

Nodes: each participant in the Bitcoin network runs a node. They choose which software to run on this node. Most people run Bitcoin Core, the main implementation of the Bitcoin protocol that was started by Satoshi and is now developed by hundreds of independent developers and companies all over the world. If this software implementation became malicious and tried to introduce something like inflation, then nobody would run it. Examples of nodes include those run by anyone who accepts Bitcoin: merchants, exchanges, wallet providers, and everyday people using Bitcoin for whatever purpose they want.

Miners: some nodes also mine, minting bitcoins, recording transactions, and making it very expensive for someone to tamper with the ledger. If the miners are the only ones who write to the ledger, it might be tempting to think of them as the rule makers, but they are not. They are simply following the rules set by the nodes that accept bitcoins. If the miners start producing blocks that contain extra reward, they will not be accepted by other nodes, thus leading those coins to be worthless. Thus, every user running a node is participating in anarchic governance—they are choosing which rules the coins that they consider Bitcoin should follow, and any violation of these rules is rejected outright.

Users/Investors: users are the people who buy and sell the bitcoin currency as well as run nodes. Some users today don't run their own nodes, but rely on a node hosted by their wallet provider, where the wallet provider acts as a sort of proxy for the wants and desires of the user. Users decide the value of the coin on the open market through supply and demand. Even if the miners and exchanges were to collude and introduce some kind of radical change such as inflation, users would likely dump the currency following those rules, driving the price low and putting the offending companies out of business. An intolerant minority of users could keep their own version of Bitcoin alive that still followed the original rules.

Developers: the Bitcoin Core software is the most popular Bitcoin client project. It has attracted a rich ecosystem of hundreds of the best crypto developers and companies. The Core project is very conservative as the software powers a network that now secures more than $100 billion. Each idea for a major change goes through a process called a Bitcoin Improvement Proposal[1] and any code changes are carefully peer-reviewed. The process for proposals and code review is done completely in the open. Anyone can join, comment, or submit code. If the developers become malicious and introduce something that nobody wants to run, then users would simply run different software. Perhaps they would stay on older versions, or start developing something new. Because of this, the core developers must develop changes that users would generally want, or risk losing their status as the reference implementation if no one wants to run it.

Rule Changing Forks

Hopefully by now you've got a good handle on how the Bitcoin software enforces the rules that people have agreed to, and how people can decide which software to run in order to enforce the rules that they believe in.

Miners decide the rules they will follow when producing blocks, but they must mine the kind of blocks that users want, or risk their blocks not being accepted and thus lose their mining reward.

We also know that the Bitcoin software will accept the heaviest valid cumulative Proof of Work chain as One True Chain, and that forks sometimes occur naturally due to the chance of simultaneous block production.

Because of the vast diversity of participants in the network, the rules of Bitcoin have been close to set in stone from the beginning. The only upgrades that have been made to Bitcoin so far have been made in a backward-compatible way, preserving the core consensus rules for non-upgraded nodes.

Now let's talk about how the rules can change. An intentional fork is when some users and/or miners decide that they don't agree with the current rules of Bitcoin, and that they need to change the rules. There are two types of rule-changing forks that have been shown in the wild: soft-forks, which are backwards compatible, and hard-forks, which are not backwards compatible. Let's go through how these occur in theory, and then look at historical examples.[2]

A *soft-fork* is a backwards compatible change in the consensus rules of Bitcoin that tightens the rules. This means that if you run an old node that has not upgraded to the new rules, your node will still see the blocks produced under the new rules as valid. Let's look at an example to make it clear.

On Sep 12, 2010, a new rule was introduced to the software: blocks must be at most 1MB in size. This rule was introduced to deal with spam in the blockchain. Prior to this rule, all blocks of any size were valid. With the new rule, only smaller blocks were valid, so the rules were tightened. If you were running an old node and didn't upgrade, then the new smaller blocks were still valid under your rules, so you were not affected.

A soft-fork is a non-disruptive way to upgrade the system because it allows node operators to upgrade to the new software slowly over time, voluntarily. If they don't upgrade, they'll still be able to process all the blocks coming in as they always did. Only the miners that produce the blocks have to upgrade to start producing blocks using the new rules. Once miners upgraded to the 1MB soft-fork, all blocks from that point on were a max 1MB in size. Users running old versions of the software were none the wiser.

In the case of a *hard-fork*, a non-backwards-compatible change is introduced. A hard fork is a ruleset expansion in which blocks that were originally invalid are now considered valid. Old nodes that did not upgrade will not be able to process the blocks produced under the new rules because they will consider them invalid. Thus they will be stuck on the old chain unless they upgrade to the new rules.

Hard forks that have near unanimous agreement from every node in the network would not cause problems. Every node would upgrade immediately to the new rules. If some stragglers were left behind, they would not get any new block updates and would, in theory, notice that their software stopped working and be forced to upgrade.

In practice, hard forks never go quite so smoothly. In a truly decentralized anarchic system, you cannot coerce everyone to change to new rules. In August 2017, some people were not happy with how the Bitcoin chain was progressing with regard to cheap payments. They decided that they wanted to fork to create a chain with larger blocks. Bitcoin had a rule about blocks being no more than 1MB, due to a soft-fork that had occurred in 2010. Some people wanted to create a new chain with larger blocks. This fork became known as Bitcoin Cash.

An out-of-consensus hard fork like Bitcoin Cash, which is not followed by all miners and nodes, creates a new blockchain. This chain shares history with the original chain including the existing UTXO set (account balances) up to the point of the fork. However, from the split point onwards, coins created on the fork are no longer Bitcoin as they are not accepted by any nodes on the Bitcoin network.

The subject what *is* or *is not* Bitcoin was hotly debated in the year following the Bitcoin Cash fork. There were some people on the Bitcoin Cash side who thought Bitcoin should be defined by what's written in the original design paper Satoshi produced ten years ago. They cherry-picked specific words from the Bitcoin white paper to prove their point. But consensus-based systems do not work by appeals to authority. They work by the collective actions of lots of individuals including choosing which software to run, and which coin to buy or sell on the open market.

In the case of this fork, the people running the vast majority of nodes —that is wallets, exchanges, merchants, and others did not want to change their software for something supported by a much smaller and less experienced development team, with a much smaller amount of hash rate securing it. Nor did people feel that such an "upgrade" was worth the disruption to the ecosystem. The problem with hard forks is that they only succeed when everyone switches. If there are stragglers, two coins are created. Thus, Bitcoin remained Bitcoin, and Bitcoin Cash became a separate coin. Since everyone who held Bitcoin prior to the fork was granted Bitcoin Cash free of charge, many people sold the coin for "free money" which further drove its price down.

Today, dozens of other forks of Bitcoin exist, such as Bitcoin SV (itself a fork of Bitcoin Cash), Bitcoin Gold, Bitcoin Diamond, and Bitcoin Private. All of them have a tiny bit of hash rate securing them, little developer activity, and nearly nonexistent on-chain activity and exchange liquidity. Their lack of liquidity makes them prime targets for pump and dumps, often leading to meteoric rises in price with equally spectacular and devastating drops. Many have been subject to wallet hacks, 51% attacks, and other disasters. Some are outright scams or simply fodder for gamblers. Most have a high degree of centralization in some aspect of their design. The website forkdrop.io is currently tracking 74 Bitcoin-wannabes.

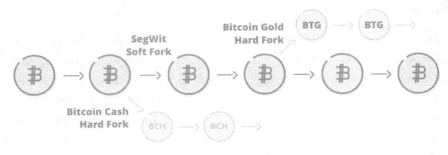

Coins from a soft-fork can be sent to older nodes. A hard-fork produces new backward-incompatible UTXOs that will not be accepted by old nodes.

Many more coins use similar code but started their ledgers from scratch without inheriting Bitcoin's UTXO set, such as Litecoin or Dogecoin. They are not typically considered Bitcoin forks even though they may share a lot of the same code because they do not share its account balance history.

A Bitcoin fork does not affect the 21 million supply limit of Bitcoin itself. Imagine you have the world's gold stored in the ultra securely engineered Fort Knox under heavy armed guard. You build a small, poorly engineered shack and call it Fort Knox Lite, securing it with a single guard. You paint some rocks a gold color and put them in the shack. You then announce to the world that you've "forked gold" and issued every holder of gold an equivalent amount of free rocks inside your shack.

We need lots of miners guarding Bitcoin, making it expensive to 51% attack. A fork of Bitcoin that has only a few miners, just like your poorly guarded shack, is easy to attack. The code is probably structurally unsound, built by a small inexperienced team of developers with poor peer review, just like your shack. Forked coins aren't accepted by any existing nodes because they break the rules of Bitcoin. Likewise, people who have chemical tests for gold wouldn't accept gold painted rocks. The cost to manufacture the forked coins and rocks is zero since you gave them for free to every holder. This limits the market's interest in forks of Bitcoin.

As you consider the thousands of Bitcoin clones that have been created, none of which have significant market value, ponder this paradox: creating Bitcoin forks is free and easy. However, changing the rules of Bitcoin or creating new bitcoins is anything but easy. Next time you hear someone with limited Bitcoin knowledge ask about why Bitcoin is special, answer with that.

The decentralized nature of the Bitcoin ecosystem creates a strong preference for the status quo. Big changes take months or years of consensus building, discussion, and peer review to implement. This is a good thing, and something we should want from a system that aims to be global money. Bitcoin is a delicate dance between thousands of participants, all of which are acting selfishly, often with competing needs. It's a truly free-market anarchist system with no one in particular in charge.

1. Read more on how Bitcoin Core's development process is managed in *Who Controls Bitcoin Core?* by Jameson Lopp: https://medium.com/@lopp/who-controls-bitcoin-core-c55c0af91b8a
2. A full history of Bitcoin rule changing forks is analyzed here https://blog.bitmex.com/bitcoins-consensus-forks/

9
WHAT'S NEXT?

Is Bitcoin the MySpace of Crypto?

Why did I write a book about Bitcoin when I could have written about the crypto ecosystem at large? Aren't there thousands of other coins? What makes Bitcoin so special, besides being the first decentralized cryptocurrency? Isn't it slower and less feature rich than all the newer competitors?

This is often asked by people new to Bitcoin. After understanding the basics of how Bitcoin works, the next logical question tends to be: "Blockchain tech sounds interesting. How do we know a better version won't show up and turn Bitcoin into the MySpace of crypto?"

A moat is a competitive advantage a business builds that prevents new entrants from easily competing. For MySpace that moat was a huge user base with friend relationships. People wouldn't use competing services if their friends weren't already there. But as large a moat as a well connected social graph is, it wasn't enough to stop Facebook from eating MySpace's lunch in the span of only a few years.

Bitcoin's moat is much, much larger than MySpace's. In order to understand that, let's examine what it would take for a Bitcoin Competitor to displace Bitcoin.

Be a more salable and liquid money

The first thing to understand is that the MySpace vs Facebook comparison is poor because you can have an account on MySpace and Facebook at the same time at no cost. This is actually what many people did during the transition phase from one to the other. Once enough critical mass was on Facebook, people stopped using MySpace.

This is not how money works, however. If you hold a dollar's worth of bitcoin, that's a a dollar's worth of another coin that you're not holding. You have to make a conscious decision to sell one currency for another. You cannot store the same value in both at the same time. Now ask yourself: why would you hold anything but the most liquid, most widely accepted currency? The answer is only speculation. If you can't shift the entire economy around you to also hold the other coin, there is no way that it can become dominant.

Bitcoin's liquidity is far beyond any of its competitors. As of today, the market cap of Bitcoin is about $160B according to https://messari.io/onchainfx. The next biggest competitor, Ethereum, has only $30B of market cap. This doesn't even measure the true liquidity by looking at how much you could meaningfully sell before the price would slip significantly.

Liquidity is a snowball. Holding the most liquid money means other people want it, and this begets more liquidity. By holding anything but the most liquid money, you are actively punishing yourself while waiting for everyone else to do the same. The economic incentives do not align in favor of liquidity shifting overnight to a competitor.

Demonstrate $100B+ worth of security over ten years.

By circumstance, Bitcoin was allowed to grow from a worthless internet geek experiment that nobody cared about, to financing the purchase of a pizza for 10,000 bitcoins, to a peak price of $20k USD per bitcoin. It did all of this relatively quietly, without anyone breathing down its neck. During this time, it built up a world class immune system from years of attacks, and grew the largest network of hash power in the world. For ten years, and securing more than 100 billion dollars, it has been impossible to hack.

It is nearly impossible to launch a new cryptocurrency today quietly. The cat is out of the bag, and all the tricks are well known. Let's look at an alternative blockchain, EOS, worth about ~$10B at launch and worth about half of that today. It experienced a freeze two days after launch due to bugs in the code. These bugs were patched within hours with minimal oversight or review. Are you going to put $100B of value on a network like that? Maybe EOS will be around in 10 years, but by that time, Bitcoin will be 20 years old and securing trillions in value.

Thwart attacks from existing hash power

Given the thousands of coins out there using dozens of hashing algorithms, any new coins are under threat of 51% attack from existing hash power. This has already happened to Bitcoin Gold and several other coins.

A new competitor has to survive attacks by existing hash power, or use an algorithm that has no specialized ASICs. If there are no ASICs, then the system can easily be attacked by renting commodity GPUs, which are widely available. It also cannot start securing a large amount of value like EOS did on day one, which is reckless and a good way to get into centralized patching behavior. So that means they can't raise money either, but rather do a fair launch similar to Bitcoin and grow slowly in value so they can build up their security model proportionally. However, if they're growing slowly, they cannot catch up to Bitcoin's user base and liquidity due to the passage of time.

Be highly decentralized

A large part of Bitcoin's security model comes from a high degree of decentralization. This means the protocol is hard to change and thus can be trusted to honor the properties promised in its code (fixed supply, etc). This property was proven when a large number of businesses and miners got together and wanted to push a change to the block size to steer the protocol in a particular direction[1]. Their fork was rejected by users and failed spectacularly.

A competitor that's highly decentralized basically rules out any companies or teams that are founded by known people as that creates a central point of failure and coercion. It also rules out any coins willing to "move fast and break things," since you can only do that when you're centralized. Any competitor is either moving fast and gets centralized, or moving slow and can never catch up.

Attract the best developers in the world

Much like Linux created a whirlwind of activity that prevented other *Nix like systems from competing, so has Bitcoin. Every day this community grows and new companies are built on top of Bitcoin, offering new services. A competitor has to steal developer mindshare from an exponentially growing nucleus which includes dozens of companies, educational programs, and conferences.

Grow a worldwide financial network

Bitcoin is supported by hundreds of exchanges worldwide, futures and other financial derivative products at large players like the Chicago Mercantile Exchange, hundreds of hedge funds and trading desks, and a network of people who already use Bitcoin as an alternative to failed currencies like the Venezuelan Bolivar. All of these things would have to be built for a Bitcoin competitor to displace it.

Institutions like the Chicago Mercantile Exchange aren't going to list every new competitor without tons of existing exchange volume to back it. You'd have to convince businesses to accept this new competitor instead of Bitcoin. A competitor that is likely less secure, less liquid, has less competent developers, and by definition less adoption worldwide. That's a steep hill to climb.

Be a sounder money

There is a gross misunderstanding that Bitcoin is supposed to be a fast and cheap way to send money. It clearly cannot be that based on its fundamental properties involving a worldwide replicated ledger. However, Bitcoin's primary and actual demonstrated use case as a censorship resistant sound money is growing.

Anything else, such as making remittances cheaper is basically a cherry on top. Most would-be competitors still think they need to solve the fast payment use case, which is already solved by dozens of centralized companies worldwide, and solved reasonably well. And it's also being solved by the quickly growing Lightning Network on top of Bitcoin.

Competing on the sound money front requires an above-all commitment to decentralization and properties that are truly hard to change and attack. Unfortunately coins cannot compete on this front by virtue of the fact that they are built typically by centralized teams with profit motive, and not a happy accident of a slowly growing ecosystem that was built by cypherpunks.

Future Developments in Bitcoin

At this point, we've gone through inventing the protocol. Now we look to the future and cover some of the near term improvements coming to Bitcoin.

Bitcoin is a programmable money on top of which we can build lots of services. This is an entirely new concept, and we're only starting to scratch the surface of what's possible.

Lightning Network

Bitcoin has had issues with high fees as block space became more and more in demand. Today, Bitcoin is only capable of about 3 to 7 transactions per second based on the number of transactions that can fit into a block; remember, however, that each transaction can actually be a payment to hundreds of people via batching. Still, it is not enough capacity to become a global payment network.

A naive solution might be to raise the block size, and indeed several competing currencies including Bitcoin Cash have tried this approach. Bitcoin does not go this route because increasing the block size would negatively impact decentralization characteristics such as the number of nodes and how geographically dispersed they are. Even if a block size increase was possible due to improvements in hardware, there is also the issue that Bitcoin's decentralized nature means that a hard fork that tries to change the block size would cause a lot of disruption, and likely another outright split into a different coin.

A block size increase would also not really solve the problem of making Bitcoin suitable as a worldwide payment system—it simply wouldn't scale that much. Enter the Lightning Network: another protocol and set of software implementations that create off-chain Bitcoin transactions that settle periodically to the blockchain. The Lightning Network could be the topic of an entire book, but we'll discuss it briefly.

The idea of Lightning is that not every transaction needs to be recorded to the blockchain. For example, if you and I are at a bar buying drinks, we can open a bar tab and settle at the end of the night. It doesn't really make sense for us to charge our credit card for every drink as it wastes time. With Bitcoin, using the energy equivalent to that of an entire country on confirming the purchase of a coffee or beer and having this purchase recorded for all of time on thousands of computers across the world is neither scalable nor particularly good for privacy.

The Lightning Network, if successful, will improve on many of Bitcoin's downsides:

- Virtually unlimited transaction throughput. Hundreds of thousands of micro transactions could be performed and committed to the Bitcoin blockchain once as final settlement.
- Instant confirmations; no need to wait for blocks to be mined.
- Sub-penny transaction fees suitable for micropayments such as paying a penny to read a blog.
- Increased privacy. Only the parties participating in the transaction need to know about it, unlike an on-chain transaction which is broadcast to the entire world.

Lightning uses the concept of Payment Channels, which are real on-chain Bitcoin transactions that lock up some amount of Bitcoin and make it available within the Lightning Network for instant, near-free transfer. The Lightning Network is in early stages but already shows promise. You can check out a site that uses Lightning-based micropayments for articles at https://yalls.org/.

Bitcoin in Space

Bitcoin does an excellent job of being censorship resistant as it is resistant to seizure (you can carry it in your head), and resistant to censorship of transfer since it only requires one honest miner on the network to commit your transactions (and you can mine yourself).

Nonetheless, being that Bitcoin is transmitted over the Internet, it is susceptible to censorship on the network level. Authoritarian regimes that want to clamp down on activity could attempt to block Bitcoin traffic entering and leaving their country.

The Blockstream Satellite network is the first effort to route around state-level network censorship, as well as reach remote areas that may not have connections to the Internet. This satellite system allows anyone with a dish and relatively inexpensive equipment to connect and download the Bitcoin blockchain, with bi-directional communication coming soon. There are also now efforts such as TxTenna to build off-the-grid mesh networks. When coupled with a satellite connection, this kind of setup would be nearly unstoppable.

Further Research

So this is it. You've gone through the exercise of Inventing Bitcoin, and hopefully emerged on the other side of the looking glass, ready to explore further. Where do you go from here? Here are a few resources to help you explore further:

To learn more about the economics behind Bitcoin:

- *The Bitcoin Standard* by Saifedean Ammous
- *Bitcoin Investment Theses* by Pierre Rochard https://medium.com/@pierre_rochard/bitcoin-investment-theses-part-1-e97670b5389b
- *The Bullish Case for Bitcoin* by Vijay Boyapati https://medium.com/@vijayboyapati/the-bullish-case-for-bitcoin-6ecc8bdecc1
- For kids: *Bitcoin Money* by Michael Caras

To get deeper on the computer science:

- *The Bitcoin Whitepaper* by Satoshi https://bitcoin.org/bitcoin.pdf
- *Mastering Bitcoin* by Andreas Antonopoulos
- *Programming Bitcoin* by Jimmy Song
- Jimmy Song's seminar at https://programmingblockchain.com

To get deeper on the history and philosophy of Bitcoin:

- *Planting Bitcoin* by Dan Held https://medium.com/@danhedl/planting-bitcoin-sound-money-72e80e40ff62,

- *Bitcoin Governance* by Pierre Rochard https://medium.com/@pierre_rochard/bitcoin-governance-37e86299470f
- *Bitcoin Past and Future* by Murad Mahmudov https://blog.usejournal.com/bitcoin-past-and-future-45d92b3180f1
- Every video made by Andreas Antonopoulos, especially *Currency Wars* and *The Monument of Immutability*, at https://www.youtube.com/user/aantonop

A huge part of the Bitcoin ecosystem lives on Twitter. Here's a handful of folks in no particular order that are good to follow. Start here, and branch out:

```
@lopp
@pwuille
@adam3us
@danheld
@TraceMayer
@pierre_rochard
@bitstein
@theonevortex
@AlenaSatoshi
@WhatBitcoinDid
@stephanlivera
@TheBlock__
@TheLTBNetwork
@real_vijay
@jimmysong
@Excellion
@starkness
@dickerson_des
@roasbeef
@saifedean
@Melt_Dem
@_jillruth
```

```
@giacomozucco
@Snyke
@aantonop
@MustStopMurad
@danheld
@peterktodd
@dergigi
@skwp (that's me)
```

You can find more of my writing at yanpritzker.com. See you on the other side.

---

1. Read more about the so-called Segwit2X fork which was planned through backroom agreements and subsequently called off here: https://bitcoinmagazine.com/articles/now-segwit2x-hard-fork-has-really-failed-activate

ACKNOWLEDGMENTS

Thank you to the many people who gave me feedback during early drafts of this book; in particular: Joe Levering, Phil Geiger, Yury Pritzker, Jonathan Wheeler, Walter Rosenberg, Michael Santosuosso, and David Harding.

Thank you to Jimmy Song for the Programming Blockchain seminar, which gave me the swift kick in the ass I needed to put this text together.

ABOUT THE AUTHOR

Yan Pritzker has been a developer and startup entrepreneur for the last 20 years. Most recently, he was the co-founding CTO at Reverb.com where he ran technology and infrastructure from 2012-2018. Today he is focused on Bitcoin education and consulting for early stage startups.

Yan writes on Bitcoin and related topics at yanpritzker.com.

You can also follow him on Twitter: @skwp.